WHY INTRANETS GET STUCK AND HOW TO FIX THEM

*by Tracy Beverly,
Susan O'Neill and
Edward Walter*

Published by Good Dog Press
A subsidiary of Strategy Studio

Good Dog Press
350 Seventh Avenue
Suite 404
New York, NY 10001

ISBN: 978-0-9832346-1-6

Design and production by Strategy Studio, New York, New York.

intranetsunstuck.com

DEDICATION

To all those who've at any point in their career committed themselves to developing or managing an organizational intranet for
the good of their employees and their companies. They understand the politics, the challenges, the complexity and the rapid
change involved in making something like an intranet worthwhile.
Likewise we dedicate this book to those who unexpectedly, in the
midst of another career, found themselves learning about designing navigation and page layouts and became passionate about
the user experience and the quality of content when they least
expected it.

TABLE OF CONTENTS

Introduction

Fixing an Intranet
That's Stuck

This short book is the result of nearly two decades of working with dozens of organizations struggling to bring their intranets to full potential. In it, the authors share 60-plus years of experience designing, developing, launching and managing intranets, portals and other internal online tools. Our goal here is to offer pragmatic strategies and tools to help you maximize the business value of your intranet.

Over the last twenty years, we've identified common themes for why Intranets get stuck. This book outlines each reason and addresses it with practical and easy-to-understand solutions.

When an intranet hasn't been adopted into the organization as fully as expected, management often questions its value. This can cause the intranet to get stuck: implemented, somewhat useful but not viewed as a strategic priority or a primary online destination for employees.

But, when done right, an intranet can be a place where users go and easily get current information, complete tasks, interact with colleagues and collaborate to get a job done. It can also be an important vehicle for communicating and reinforcing corporate culture and messages.

The central question this book addresses is why your intranet has not reached its potential and what you can do to improve the situation.

We may answer this question differently than other business and technology books you've read. We decided not to use case studies, as these tend to lengthen a book without much direct, practical benefit to the reader. Instead, we identify key causes for intranets not reaching their potentials, and then offer solutions you can use to make your intranet employees' resource of choice.

Who should read this book
This book is written for managers, department or division heads, and those who have responsibility for their organization's intranet. Really, it's for anyone who wants to make the organization's intranet better than it is now.

While this is a book about intranets, it is not about technology; it is not written for IT professionals. While we do cover technology at a high level, we believe a successful intranet is about much more than code, legacy platforms and off-the-shelf intranet products.

Even though this book focuses on practical advice for improving an existing intranet, it is also useful for those who are tasked to start their organization's first intranet. It will help you think through the roadmap for creating an intranet and alert you to common pitfalls that can derail an internal online effort before it has even been released.

How to use this book

There are four sections. The first identifies the ten most common causes intranets fail. As you read chapter one, take note of reasons that match your organization's situation.

The second section covers the nine critical areas where organizations need to focus their efforts to get their intranet back on track. In this section, each chapter concentrates on a single area such as strategy, users or communications.

The third section sums up our view on the characteristics of a best-in-class intranet – the ultimate goal all organizations can strive for and achieve.

These first three sections are full of diagrams and sidebars that not only make the book easy to read, but useful, as they contain practical advice you can implement.

The book has a companion website, www.intranetsunstuck. com. The site houses tools and templates you can download and use. These are materials the authors have developed and used in working with organizations large and small. The site also includes documents too long to include in the book that you can download in their entirety. The login process is simple and free, and you can download and share items as many times as you'd like.

We hope you'll find the information and insights in this book helpful and that you will be able to apply the tips and tools to maximize the effectiveness of your intranet.

Ed Walter, Tracy Beverly and Susan O'Neill

TWENTY QUESTIONS THAT COULD CHANGE YOUR INTRANET

Rate Your Intranet: Take the following quiz, add up your scores and see if your organization's intranet is trying, succeeding, or award-winning. Or take the quiz online at intranetsunstuck.com

1. The mission of your intranet is to:
   A. Reduce help desk calls.
   B. Support cost management by delivering key administrative systems to employees.
   C. Provide all employees with a shared virtual company home and consolidated workspace.

2. The best way to characterize employee usage of the intranet is:
   A. Rarely used.
   B. Used to get access to a few critical databases or applications.
   C. Used several times per workweek by the majority of employees.

3. The best description of your intranet's user experience is:
   A. Worth the hunt – if persistent, employees will find what they want.
   B. Generally good in most places.
   C. Consistently successful across the site.

4. Your intranet is championed by:
   A. The IT department, the intranet owner and team.
   B. Human Resources and/or Communications.
   C. Senior management and employees.

5. Your intranet's home page includes:
   A. A collection of unrelated static boxes.
   B. Company news, frequently used resources, a home base for site-wide navigation and content structure.
   C. Today's company and employee news, including stock quotes, photos from employee events, and obituaries, in addition to frequently used resources and active navigation.

6. The content on your intranet includes:
   A. Directories, IT applications and content that is publicly available elsewhere.
   B. Directories, company information, policies and forms, human resources and benefits information and travel/procurement information.
   C. Directories, company information, policies and forms, HR and benefits information, travel/procurement information, access to key administrative systems, emergency management instructions, online communications and learning, knowledge management and local-office and departmental sites.

7. The best way to describe the technology supporting your intranet is:
   A. Vintage.
   B. The best of the previous decade.
   C. A series of connected tools designed for web platforms in a social media world.

8. User complaints about your intranet most often focus on:
   A. Speed, access and authentication issues; finding content; "knowing it's there but not knowing where."
   B. Finding content, the quality or freshness of the content, ineffective search engine.
   C. Finding a home page story from a vacation week, the time lag to post a submittal, intranet content not local enough, can't access from my mobile device.

9. Your intranet team is made up of:
   A. Me and some people with day jobs.
   B. A small dedicated team that coordinate with content managers across the organization and are supplemented by consultants for redesigns and new functionality implementations.
   C. A dedicated team, including editorial, search, metrics and social media positions, that has relationships with key vendors, producers or project managers who coordinate with content managers across the organization and support them in meeting business needs.

10. Your intranet team's approach to improving user experience includes:
   A. User training and documentation.
   B. User surveys, employee interviews, card sorting.
   C. Front to back multi-site user experience testing, including authentication, search, navigation, content findability, design; regular surveys; ongoing feedback management; an employee advisory group.

11. Conversations with senior management about your intranet tend to sound like this:
   A. "The intranet is not the same as the public website" or maybe "Is there still a company intranet?"
   B. "Our latest survey results show that our employees most use . . . , they need . . . "
   C. "Your discussion of Q1 results will be posted". . . , "We've enabled Twitter on the emergency response module", "Our plan to integrate the newly acquired division is . . ."

12. Your intranet budget for next year includes the following areas of investment:
   A. Investment?
   B. Better search engine and metrics package, usability research, editorial resources.
   C. A web content management system supporting distributed authorship and targeting, integrated social media components, dedicated search and metrics resources and a social media coordinator.

13. Intranet standards management in your organization includes:
   A. A panic button and rapid take-down response.
   B. Basic guidelines codified and shared with content managers.
   C. Standards and guidelines approved by the governance board, available on the intranet for all content managers and employees, with regular compliance reviews and updates.

14. Your intranet's governing body is:
    A. Informal.
    B. Chaired by a strong intranet sponsor and includes key stakeholders.
    C. Chaired by a strong intranet sponsor, includes key stakeholders across the organization, and is guided by an agreed governance charter outlining decision making processes and roles.

15. Measuring the effectiveness of your intranet focuses on:
    A. Uptime, total hits.
    B. Unique visitors, page visits, performance metrics.
    C. Analyzing a wide range of interrelated metrics including usage trends, content activity, system performance and user feedback.

16. Search
    A. Employees tend not to use search because the results are rarely useful.
    B. Search is reasonably good for content that is commonly searched for but not very effective for other types of searches.
    C. Search results are consistently relevant and accurate.

17. Content management
    A. Basic with little distributed capabilities or templates to support consistency.
    B. Some distributed capabilities; inconsistent tagging of pages for ownership and date last updated.
    C. Fully distributed authorship and approvals based on shared templates and standards, supported by an automated page expiration system.

18. Social media
    A. There's been lots of wishful thinking but no plans and no funding.
    B. We've done some pilots but have no overall strategy or agreement on goals and success measures.
    C. A strategy and plan have been developed and we are in the first phase of execution. Senior management understands that these are capabilities to add into the mix, not silver bullets.

19. Mobile capabilities
    A. Why would we need a mobile intranet?
    B. The home page looks okay on mobile devices.
    C. A lite version is customized for mobile devices, with easy access to people and location searches, company news and
    announcements, and key applications such as time sheets.

20. Future/ongoing improvement
    A. Once the intranet was rolled out, very little has been done to improve or enhance it.
    B. We have been able to make incremental improvements in response to feedback received from users and content owners. We have funded these improvements through the normal operating budget.
    C. We have continued to invest in the intranet and have been able to enhance the user experience, upgrade the technology tools and introduce new features into the intranet.

How did you do?
Give yourself, 10 points for every C, 7 for every B, and 5 for every A.

Your total points: (based on 20 questions) _____

Total Points

Trying 100-135   Give your organization credit for trying, but a lot of things need to change for you to succeed. Bring in some outside help and start again.

Succeeding 136-170   Congratulations, your intranet is succeeding–but could be so much more.

Award-Winning > 170 Points   You've got a terrific intranet! Submit it for awards, congratulate your team, thank your third-party partners, survey your employees, and look to the future.

Stuck

10 Reasons Why Intranets Fail

Intranet technology and strategies have been around for more than a decade, and lots of organizations have some type of intranet at this point. In many cases, they are on their second or even third iteration, hoping that newer technology, social media or a new "killer" application will increase employee usage and help the intranet achieve the promised ROI. But often these objectives are not achieved, and organizations can't figure out what they are doing wrong or should be doing differently.

There are quite a few ways an intranet can get stuck and not reach its potential. If yours is stuck, the reasons below may help you recognize your organization's issues. If you don't know how good your intranet is, answer our "20 questions that could change your intranet" quiz on page 11 to see just where it stands.

Reason 1: The goals are not well defined

All too often intranet projects are begun without clear strategic objectives. Sometimes organizations believe they can reduce operational costs, but are not clear about exactly how. Or, sometimes organizations become convinced they need an intranet because a competitor has one, or because a persuasive intranet technology vendor has convinced them of the need. All too often in these situations the organization is unclear about what it should expect from an intranet. Starting this way can only lead to disappointment.

Another very common problem is the "Field of Dreams" misunderstanding – "build it and they will come." In these situations organizations believe all they need to do is put the infrastructure in place and somehow the intranet will grow organically. The organic growth never happens.

Reason 2: Ownership is not clear

Ownership is a significant issue for intranets because they typically touch so many parts of an organization. It's not always clear what role various business units–whether Information Technology, Human Resources, Communications or Knowledge Management–should have in the intranet strategy, or how best to set priorities and resolve conflicts. The lack of clarity can lead to interdepartmental battles for dominance, or leave an intranet with no owner because no one wants to assume responsibility. Conflict can also arise where there is an acquisition or a merger, and there are competing intranets and no clear strategy for consolidation and governance.

Another significant issue is the level of sponsorship. Senior leadership does not always see the importance of providing visible support for an intranet strategy, and that leaves the door open for business units to go their own way. Also, a lack of senior leadership support sends the wrong message to employees about the intranet's value.

Reason 3: Departments try to do it alone

The idea to implement an intranet can be hatched in a variety of departments. In many situations it starts with IT; either they have been told by leadership to implement intranet technology or IT sees the advantages of the technology and tries to push the intranet forward. All too often this is perceived as a solution looking for a problem (as opposed to the other way around), and it doesn't work out.

In other instances, a particular department or business unit recognizes a need and then tries to solve the problem on its own without consulting with other parts of the organization. This type of siloed thinking can seem reasonable in the beginning – a single business unit can address its specific requirements more quickly – but in the long run this approach ill serves the needs of the overall organization and undermines the potential of the intranet. Most importantly, this path doesn't address the needs of employees who have to interact with all parts of the business, not just one department.

When business units try to move forward with an intranet strategy on their own, they typically find it harder with each passing year to evolve and upgrade the intranet. In addition, there usually is little integration with other systems because it's too difficult for an individual business unit to make this happen. That limits the intranet's evolution and makes for a poor user experience.

Reason 4: Users and their needs are neglected
An intranet project that starts by analyzing what user experience employees want is the rare exception. Usually it's all about what the organization wants to communicate or make accessible, or how the technology works; the user experience is an afterthought.

Most organizations underestimate user expectations when they start an intranet project and then aren't equipped to keep pace as expectations evolve. This is an especially difficult issue for organizations whose intranets were introduced several years ago, and whose technology and user experience haven't kept up with what employees experience with other web sites or web-based tools.

Many organizations also fail to look at the whole user experience. It's not just about the intranet itself – it's about logging in, the speed and performance of the intranet and supporting systems, and flexibility of access. The user experience is undermined if it's too complicated to log in because of security concerns or a lack of system integration. If the speed is very slow or performance is poor, employees will avoid the intranet – using it costs them time and impacts their productivity. If the intranet is not accessible via mobile devices or to employees working remotely, it's outside the critical path for employees and won't be used regularly.

Also, it's important to keep in mind that the definition of an employee has changed over the last few years, and many intranets haven't adjusted their access and security policies to accommodate the changes. Today most organizations have different types of employee relationships (outsourced employees, contractors, joint ventures, offshore employees, etc.), and if the intranet is not accessible to all these employees, a significant portion of the user population is being ignored, limiting the full potential of the intranet.

Reason 5: Mistaken belief that technology is a silver bullet

Many organizations embark on an intranet project based on the false belief that the only important decision is picking the right technology. They focus all their attention on identifying IT requirements and fail to gather other requirements, think about what it will take to implement an intranet, or plan for ongoing management and support needs. Technology alone, even with the best possible platform, is never a silver bullet.

When an organization focuses exclusively on technology for its intranet, it's common to assume that the IT department should drive the project. This often leads to several problems: a lack of ownership and buy-in from other business units; disconnectedness from the needs of users and content owners; and inadequate understanding by the business of implementation requirements.

One final point. When the focus is on finding the ideal intranet platform, it is easy to lose sight of the need to integrate with other legacy systems. This can make it hard to meet critical requirements like single sign-on and seamless access to other systems, both internal and external.

Reason 6: Content is an afterthought

A very common issue that gets an intranet stuck is insufficient focus on content. There's often a naive belief that the content elements of the intranet strategy will require little effort. Thus, many intranet projects don't start planning for the content elements early enough. This leads to several problems: not enough content when the intranet is launched, or inclusion of irrelevant, out-of-date, or poorly prepared content, making search and organization difficult. All this undermines employees' first impression, and can leave them believing that the intranet is not very useful and not to be trusted.

Even if an intranet project includes initial content planning, there is often no strategy or process for maintaining and enhancing content once it's live. The content quickly gets old and loses its value.

Identifying good content for an intranet and working with the content owners to clean, tag, and prepare it takes time, and too many organizations underestimate the level of complexity and effort involved. Some content owners also want to dictate how their content is used, and this can lead to problems with how the content aligns with the intranet's information architecture and how it integrates with search functionality.

Reason 7: Intranet resources are insufficient or the wrong kind

A lot of intranets are poorly managed and staffed because organizations underestimate what's needed to perform this function effectively. Typically, they focus on IT resourcing – on what is needed to run the infrastructure and supporting systems – but not on the other resources needed to manage the user experience and the content, or to stimulate usage and nurture online community activities. Relatively few intranet teams have the right mix and depth of resources.

Often little thought is given to the skills needed to be an effective intranet leader. Some organizations pluck someone from IT or one of the sponsoring business units to lead the intranet team regardless of whether that individual has the right experience to do the job. This can be a recipe for failure, especially if the leader chosen does not have experience managing stakeholders or negotiating through conflicting demands from business units.

Another common mistake is not making the intranet leader position senior enough. If the leader is too low in the organizational hierarchy, his or her ability to drive strategy, influence stakeholders and set priorities is significantly weakened.

Reason 8: The intranet's rollout was a secret

Many organizations underestimate the level, volume and scope of communications necessary to build awareness and usage of the intranet when it is first introduced. This is also true in situations where an intranet has been re-launched or significantly enhanced. Often, communications consist of an email blast, a mention in the employee newsletter, and a couple of posters in the coffee room. These barely have an impact on employee awareness and aren't the kind of promotion needed to stimulate and grow usage.

Building awareness and usage takes time and ongoing encouragement. This requires a sustained communications campaign, and many organizations don't plan for this. There is little to no follow-up after the initial launch efforts. The intranet communications team naively expects employees to figure out for themselves what's on the intranet and how it can help them do their jobs better.

Reason 9: Mistaken belief that launch means the project is done

The intranet's launch means the project is done, right? That's a mistake many organizations make – thinking the project is complete once the intranet has been released. This mindset is often found in situations where the focus has been on getting the technology platform in place. The IT department may be right in defining *its* project as complete, but if the business doesn't understand that much more is needed to gain employee acceptance and to maintain the intranet, it has failed before it even had a chance to take root.

It is a major error to assume that the hard work is done with the launch. Organizations that don't plan for what it will take to maintain content and tools, or underestimate the ongoing level of promotion and encouragement needed to embed the intranet in employees' daily processes, will not achieve a successful intranet strategy.

An intranet's success is directly tied to the commitment and level of effort after its launch. Unfortunately, too many organizations either don't understand this reality or underestimate what's needed.

Reason 10: Continuous improvement is an aspiration but not a reality

Everyone agrees with the idea of continuous improvement. Most organizations include this aspiration in their intranet strategies. The problem often is that while this concept looks good on paper, it is challenging to make happen in reality. Many organizations strive for continuous improvement, but lack funding or support to make any major enhancements once the intranet has been launched. They're limited to making small improvements around the edges. Usually that means they can't respond in meaningful ways to user feedback or keep up with trends in technology and user expectations.

When an intranet strategy can't change and evolve, the chances of sustained levels of usage and acceptance are low. Often in these situations, further investment starts to shrink. It becomes a self-fulfilling prophecy – the less the investment and commitment to continuous improvement, the less the intranet is used, and the more likely it is to fail.

A major misstep for many organizations is forgetting to honestly assess their intranet's progress against goals on a regular basis. They don't make the time for such an exercise, or it's too difficult to get all the stakeholders and business units together to complete the assessment. Regardless of the reason, neglecting to perform a regular assessment can easily lead to a loss of focus, misunderstanding about what's actually happening, and weak commitment to the future.

Is your intranet stuck? The following pages and online tools (which can be found at intranetsunstuck.com) can help.

Strategy

2

Defining Purpose
and Setting Goals

Are your intranet goals defined clearly? What's it really for? These questions can be hard to answer. More often than not, we hear vague mention of cost saving or productivity gains, rather than a focus on how the intranet will *support strategic goals*.

An intranet without a clear strategic focus has little hope of getting support from senior executives. Over time it risks being seen as a resource drain, rather than the key business tool that was intended.

When setting goals for your intranet, it's important to keep in mind both the demands of users and the needs of the business. It is a given that a key goal of any intranet is to make the lives of employees easier; but helping senior leadership communicate mission and corporate culture can be as important. There should be an overarching strategy for the intranet, not just for the individual departments it will support.

You should define a strategy and set goals for your intranet at each crucial time in its evolution. Certainly, you want a strategy when the organization first decides to launch an intranet; but there are other key junctures, including new senior leadership, an acquisition or divestiture, a new business mandate, or any other significant change in the business direction or strategy. This is critical to keeping the intranet strategy aligned with the overall priorities of the business.

Also, if your existing intranet has not met original expectations, a strategy development exercise should be the starting point for rethinking your approach.

THE ART OF BUILDING A STRATEGY

Start with a discovery process

The first step in developing a strategy is defining the intranet's primary objectives and the criteria for measuring success. It's critical to articulate how the intranet will support the key priorities of the business in areas like Human Resources, Knowledge Management, Communications and corporate culture. It is also important to know who the key stakeholders are, and understand their business priorities and expectations of the intranet.

A step often overlooked is an honest assessment of the current state. You'll need to review questions like user population and demographics, usage patterns and key content/applications. In the case of a new intranet, an analysis of existing tools (features, user base and usage levels) that provide the functionality envisioned should be a priority. You need to understand employees' allegiances and preferences, as well as the biggest pain points in the current situation, in order to address them effectively in your intranet strategy.

Well-considered intranet projects start with a user needs analysis–another critical element of the discovery process. This could include:

- Reviewing employee feedback questions and trouble tickets for the existing intranet or similar tools.

- Conducting research using both qualitative and quantitative methods. This doesn't need to be costly – you can learn a lot from a handful of focus group sessions combined with online surveys.

- Reviewing the use of distribution channels including mobile phones and social networking.

No intranet, particularly in its first phases, can address all user needs; so it's crucial to ascertain the functionality and content/applications that will garner the most user enthusiasm.

If you're integrating multiple intranets, it's also important to understand what is critical to employees using each intranet being integrated, as well as what improvements would help convince users that the change to an integrated intranet is worthwhile.

A technology assessment should also be part of your discovery process. It's key to understand IT's strategic direction and how that aligns with the intranet's needs.

Be realistic: while it makes sense to push the envelope with your IT department, don't fall into the trap of developing a "pipedream" strategy that's impossible for IT to support. You'll end up with a permanent gap between your stated goals and what you are able to deliver.

The discovery process should also include gaining an understanding of the internal communications channels available to help you promote the intranet. If there is an existing intranet, it is important to understand what was done in the past and with what results. Building user awareness and enthusiasm early in the life cycle of the intranet is critical to achieving your goals, so it's very important to get this element of the strategy right.

A final step in discovery is taking a step back and assessing the most significant challenges and how these can be addressed. They will be different for each organization, but it is critical to understand them and think through how they can be overcome.

Pages 38 and 39 outline a detailed Strategy Development Guide. This document can also be found online at intranetsunstuck.com.

✦ Strategy Development Guide

Discovery Tasks	Types of Questions
Development of intranet strategy	• Who should participate in the development of the intranet strategy? • How will you get buy-in and agreements?
Review of project objectives and critical success criteria	• What are primary objectives of the new intranet? • What are the highest priorities to be achieved in the first year? • What are the criteria for measuring success? • What is the business context for the intranet strategy?

Stakeholder analysis
  Brand
  Human Resources
  Communications
  Knowledge
  Management
  Information Technology
  Others
	• Who are the key stakeholders?
	• For each stakeholder:
	  – What are their business priorities or hot buttons that the intranet can support?
	  – What are their expectations for the intranet?
	  – What content, applications or collaboration tools do they have on the intranet or plan to have?

Current-state assessment – analysis of current intranet environment
  User population and demographics
  Usage patterns
  Key content and applications
	• What content, applications or collaboration tools are available on the current intranet (or intranets if there are more than one); or what similar tools will be replaced by the intranet?
	• Who uses the current intranet?
	• What is the frequency of usage?
	• How do users access the intranet?
	• What content, applications or collaboration tools are used most often?
	• What usage metrics are tracked; how are they used?

User needs analysis	• What feedback have users provided about the current intranet?
	• What are the gaps in content, applications and collaboration tools?
	• What can be improved about the user experience?
	• What new functionality should the intranet have?
	• What distribution channels beyond the intranet are being considered (e.g., extranet, mobile, social media)?
	• What issues or gaps do stakeholders want addressed?
	• If there are multiple intranets, what needs to be integrated?
Technology analysis	• What is the current state?
	• What key features and functionality are needed to support the new intranet strategy?
	• What is the strategic direction for IT overall, what are IT's key objectives, and how should the intranet strategy align with them?
	• How will you manage ongoing maintenance and enhancements?
Communications analysis	• What internal communications channels are available to promote the intranet?
	• What has been done in the past to promote the intranet? How successful has this been?
	• How will the communications strategy for the intranet align with larger communications objectives (for example, a new brand rollout)?
Assessment of project implementation challenges	• What are the potential obstacles to successful implementation?
	• How can these obstacles be addressed?
	• What is the single most important project goal to be achieved?

Strategy development should be collaborative
You can't develop an effective strategy in isolation.
Involving stakeholders and leadership in the process
increases their understanding and their commitment.
It also helps to ensure that the intranet strategy is
closely linked with business goals and priorities.

The strategy development process doesn't need to be
complicated or lengthy. With the knowledge gathered
during the discovery process, it can be relatively easy to
design a collaborative process to:

• Agree on purpose.

• Set goals and priorities.

• Define approach.

• Develop a plan and road map.

The collaborative analysis and synthesis, facilitated
by an internal resource or a third party, will involve a
series of meetings or workshops to assess the knowledge gleaned from the discovery phase. It will also
ensure that all participants in strategy development
have a common understanding of the existing situation.
This sets the stage for an analysis of current strengths
and weaknesses as well as opportunities and threats to
address in the strategy. It is a multi-step process, as it

takes time to review the information from the discovery stage, answer everyone's questions and agree what it all means. Once the analysis is completed, it's important to have a frank discussion of its implications and reach consensus about the way forward.

The implementation of your intranet strategy will be much easier and have a higher chance of success if stakeholders have a common understanding of the strategy and agree on goals and success criteria. Spend the time up front with stakeholders to make this happen – in the long run, it will pay off in a big way.

Intranet Strategy Development

Discovery Intelligence	Collaborative Analysis and Synthesis	Recommendations
Review of Objectives		Strategy and Plan
Stakeholder Assessment	SWOT Analysis	Strategy
Current State Assessment	Strengths	Project plan
Needs Assessment	Weaknesses	Phases
Communications Assessment	Opportunities	Timeline
Technology Assessment	Threats	Resourcing
Implementation Challenges Assessment		Rollout

THE NEED FOR SPONSORSHIP AND GOVERNANCE

Why ownership is key

One of the main reasons intranets fail is because of weak, isolated or nonexistent sponsorship. Without an official sponsor and recognition, an intranet will be a great idea, a popular solution, a short-term wonder created by someone with too much time, or by a team looking to survive in the organization.

An intranet needs a high-level advocate and sponsor. This person is tied into management, and both makes the case for and ensures continuing alignment between the intranet and business strategy. Sponsorship should sit with and possibly rotate among the units that depend the most on the intranet – Human Resources, Knowledge Management, Strategy and Planning, Corporate Communications, or even Marketing and Business Development.

Finding the best sponsor

The sponsor should probably not be from IT. Even if the IT advocate is employee-focused and business-savvy, IT sponsorship paints the intranet as a technology "thing" and, rightly or wrongly, management and employees will never see it otherwise.

The best sponsor is supported and informed by, and accountable to, an advisory board or steering group of knowledgeable peers. This group sets strategy and budget priorities, identifies resources, and agrees on time frames. The steering group should include representation from all major stakeholders including legal, business and all geographies.

(i) Characteristics of Strong Intranet Sponsorship

- Is a champion with a direct relationship to senior management and the leadership team, usually in the department with the largest stake in the intranet, such as Corporate Communications, with direct links to other key stakeholders such as HR, IT, KM, etc.
- Drives the strategy and sets the pace.
- Keeps the intranet closely aligned with business strategy and priorities.
- Is a passionate employee advocate, whose dedication to doing right by the user is the deciding factor when groups or priorities conflict.
- Accepts the intranet's role not as an additional responsibility, but a user whose job would be impossible without the intranet.
- Makes decisions and sticks with them through implementation.
- Occasionally moves forward with an important initiative and "we will figure out how to pay for it later."
- Chairs the intranet governance board.

CHOOSING AND ESTABLISHING AN INTRANET GOVERNANCE MODEL

Centralized Governance

Some intranets have a single steering group, while others have multiple governing bodies; this largely depends on the organizational structure and industry.

Technology companies most frequently have two oversight groups, with one focusing on the content and user experience, the other on review and approval of the technology. This is most common in IT companies because intranet applications are generated throughout the organization, and deployed on central infrastructure in short-term deployment windows. The applications need to be vetted for compliance with technical and security standards before being integrated, and must be ready to get "on the train" quickly or respond effectively to upgrades and changes in the technical environment.

The technical steering or integration group also rules on major technical architectural decisions, monitors major projects and risk, oversees investment in and compliance with shared resources, and sets standards for when to develop or enhance versus using out-of-the-box technology.

Centralized Governance Model

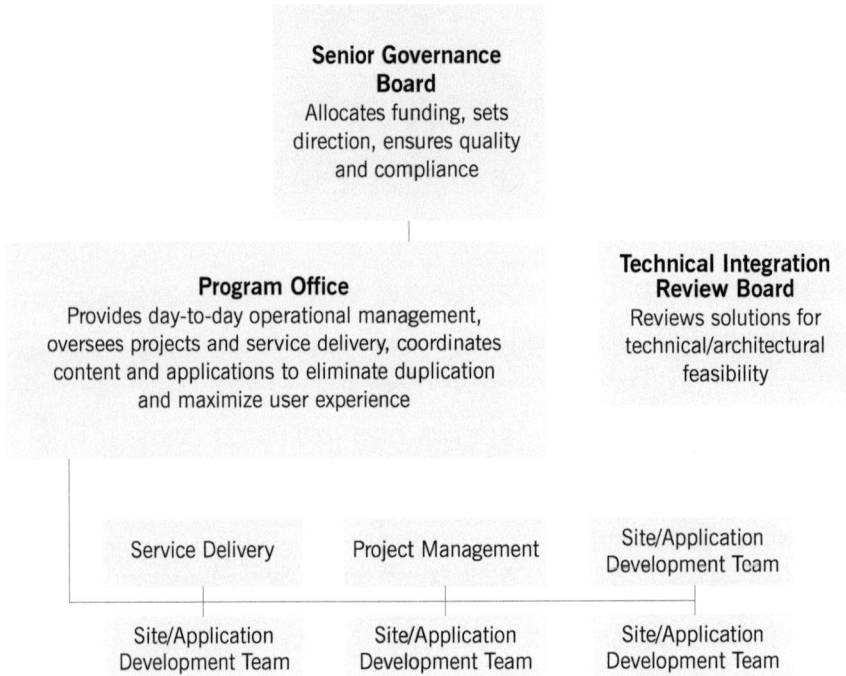

Senior Governance Board
Allocates funding, sets direction, ensures quality and compliance

Program Office
Provides day-to-day operational management, oversees projects and service delivery, coordinates content and applications to eliminate duplication and maximize user experience

Technical Integration Review Board
Reviews solutions for technical/architectural feasibility

Service Delivery

Project Management

Site/Application Development Team

Site/Application Development Team

Site/Application Development Team

Site/Application Development Team

Reporting to the governance board(s), strongly centralized intranets feature a central program office that oversees the day-to-day management of the intranet.

(i) *An Intranet Program Office*

- Manages stakeholders and steering groups, provides regular status reporting.
- Coordinates deployments and interdependencies.
- Defines and manages intranet projects and service delivery.
- Tracks issues and manages escalation and resolution.
- Defines and manages change control processes.
- Identifies needs and gaps, defines requirements for enhancements.
- Serves as user advocate, ensuring good user experience.
- Integrates content and coordinates content manager community.
- Manages shared web services and vendors such as search, metrics, multimedia hosting, feedback, and social features.
- Develops and communicates shared tool sets, best practices, standards and guidelines, training programs, system documentation.
- Manages budget, cost allocations, roles and position descriptions.
- Monitors intranet activity and quality, identifies and mitigates risks.
- Leads continuous improvement activities.

Decentralized governance

Intranets incorporating multiple divisions or countries usually have governing groups at multiple levels. There may be one for each major division or country, with rotating representation for smaller groups. These governance groups represent local business priorities, requirements and employees, protecting them from "grand schemes" that interrupt operations, waste time and money, or bring too much change at once.

Divisional and local steering groups represent local language and terminology, integrate the global intranet with local applications, ensure new applications are supported by local PCs and mobile devices, and make sure the intranet complies with local laws and processes. These groups coordinate with the global steering group to agree on which branding, navigational and taxonomy elements are shared across the intranet, and which can be more decentralized.

Decentralized Governance Model

Where does your organization score on the central-versus-decentralized governance chart? Use the diagram below to find out.

Intranet Steering Group	• Initiators of multi-year vision and plan. • Operational sign-off of business cases.
Intranet Working Group	• Development of business cases, detailed requirements. • Subject matter experts and implementation responsibilities.

Intranet Working Group Workstreams	• Power users.
	• Help generate business requirements.
	• Streams: Use tracking.
	           Rich functionality.
	           Content optimization.

The global steering group generally oversees the overall long-term intranet mission, branding, and standards for quality management, user experience, content, and technology. It is responsible for securing and maintaining stakeholder buy-in, reducing duplication of effort, ensuring that investment is spent strategically, making sure there is a clear direction on the use of tools, integrating new divisions and geographies, and decommissioning "bandit" intranets.

Well-managed governing bodies with clearly defined roles can significantly enhance an intranet. But with too many steering groups or overlapping responsibilities, "governance" can also kill an intranet, if it is unproductive or if too much bureaucracy leads to indecision or inactivity.

(i) *An Intranet Steering Group*

- Articulates or approves the multi-year vision in light of business requirements and market developments.
- Keeps intranet strategy aligned with business strategy.
- Secures and allocates funding.
- Sets priorities.
- Monitors progress against objectives.
- Approves standards and guidelines, ensures compliance.

Central versus Decentralized Governance Approach

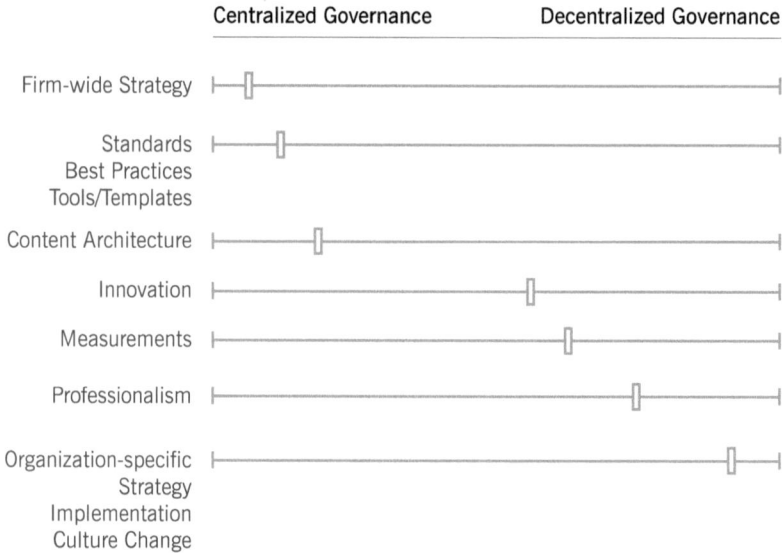

	Centralized Governance	Decentralized Governance
Firm-wide Strategy		
Standards Best Practices Tools/Templates		
Content Architecture		
Innovation		
Measurements		
Professionalism		
Organization-specific Strategy Implementation Culture Change		

Governance boards or advisory groups vary widely based on the organizational culture and the scope of the intranet. Some meet monthly, some annually. Some have permanent representation from IT, HR, Corporate Communications and Legal; some have rotating chairs and membership.

Developing the governance plan

To ensure governance is useful instead of counterproductive, successful companies develop some kind of governance agreement covering decision processes and rights. Some governance documents have a few statements outlining shared principles and roles, while others have lengthy sections outlining key decisions, those with the authority to make them, and ways employees and groups may participate in the intranet.

Vendors will sell an organization a governance plan, but these tend to be technology-specific rather than about the business of an intranet, and the sellers are almost exclusively technology consultants. No out-of-the-box plan will work without the hard work of contextualizing it to the organization and intranet. That work will need to be done by an internal resource, or a consultant who knows the organization, its business, and the intranet very well.

(i) *A Good Governance Plan*

- Defines the scope and mission of the intranet - what's in and what's out.
- Sets out guiding principles for decision making.
- Outlines policies for meeting objectives, setting priorities and managing conflicts.
- Identifies key roles and related processes.
- Approves and monitors compliance with standards and guidelines.
- Is open and accessible to all intranet participants.
- Is regularly reviewed and updated by the steering groups.

Setting intranet standards and guidelines

The governance plan is distinct from intranet standards and guidelines. The latter outline specific details on content, graphical, navigational and usability design, appropriate technical toolsets, metrics and expiration and other operational rules.

Standards and guidelines are critical. The governance board probably doesn't develop them, but it approves and oversees compliance with them. A complete outline of essential standards and guidelines can be found at www.intranetsunstuck.com.

Some final thoughts on governance

No single sponsorship or governance model will work for all intranets. Too much depends on organizational culture, intranet maturity, and technical infrastructure. The key to success is strong sponsorship, ongoing integration with key stakeholders, and a productive decision process.

DON'T DO IT ALONE

Building and maintaining an effective intranet and organizational tool is definitely a team sport. However, too often individual business units or administrative departments such as Human Resources recognize that an overall organizational strategy is lacking or that there is no strong sponsor who can champion an intranet initiative. So, looking for a better way to communicate with employees, increase staff productivity or simply fill a void, some units attempt to build an intranet themselves.

This is a daunting task in the best of circumstances. Consequently, doing it alone is rarely the first option for any unit or department. The decision generally comes after being frustrated by IT or Corporate dragging their feet, when units recognize that they are in a very decentralized or siloed environment.

IT needs to be on board

It's often with good reason that IT isn't jumping into the fray to develop an intranet. They have what they believe is a complete picture of the organization's technology infrastructure, and that infrastructure may not be scalable. Or they may simply have a full plate with their ongoing operational responsibilities, and absent a mandate from senior management, the intranet probably won't be a priority for IT.

This can lead to one or more groups trying to develop an internal online tool themselves. Typically the result is limited success, because there is no coordinated vision, no clear understanding of users' needs or limited knowledge of the technology infrastructure.

Decentralization and the sense of control

Decentralized organizations are often cultures where control is viewed as a key component for success. Divisions or business units believe their content or functionality is unique to their staff. When this idea of control is carried over to the intranet, it can lead a division or business unit to develop an intranet of its own.

Initially these one-off intranets can seem effective, given their narrow, departmental focus. However, most such intranets don't reach full potential: They lack the coordinated effort coming from all corners of the organization that makes for a robust internal online environment.

Autonomy versus consolidation

Sometimes it makes good sense to maintain some level of autonomy. There can be secure or classified information that should not be available to the entire organization or specific employee content that requires third-party intervention. However, autonomy doesn't have to come at the cost of isolation from the larger online environment. Possible strategies for consolidating all or part of your online content and functionality might include:

- Microsite strategy – This strategy creates a structure for mini-sites specific to a particular topic or function. These sites would, however, adhere to strict organization-wide conventions set up to maintain a user experience consistent with the overall intranet and to align with technology standards and practices.

- Information architecture strategy – A single intranet

with an information architecture strategy to accommodate specific department needs is possible. The
information architecture can be developed to allow a
select group of employees access, from the larger intranet, to specific sections based on their affiliations.
This strategy lets specific content be viewed by specific personnel without additional logins. For instance,
a business line can have a tab in the main navigation
of the home page that is present and accessible only
for employees in that business unit.

- Portal strategy – The portal strategy provides an
overarching information architecture and consolidated home page with the potential for flexibility at
the next level down. For example, this is an easy way
to integrate third-party content providers, such as
health and wellness sites, into the intranet.

Regardless of which of these strategies you pursue,
keep in mind that supplemental distribution outlets
like mobile apps could be used to enable employees to
perform tasks.

The underlying goal of any organization is to empower employees to make the best decisions for the company. In order to do that, employees need to be working with the most accurate information. An intranet developed in collaboration with multiple departments or divisions can provide access to the most current information the organization has to offer.

The operative word here is *collaboration*. To make the intranet truly valuable, the organization needs to bring together its business units, HR, Marketing, Legal and Administration to identify the business functions that can make the best use of an employee's time and ability.

(i) *Integration Guidelines: To Consolidate and How Much...*

Answer these questions as you consider the most effective degree
of consolidation. This can be found online at intranetsunstuck.com.

User Needs

- Are there common functions and tasks throughout the organization?
- How can access be handled throughout the organization: single url,
  common navigation, common remote login?
- Does the organization have a common language, or if not how will
  the intranet handle multiple languages?

Business Needs

- Are the objectives of the intranet common and clear throughout
  the organization?
- Where objectives differ, what would a model look like for
  consolidating them?
- What are the common tasks and who are the individuals to
  meet organizational objectives?

Control

- Is control over content, functionality, and/or technology better
  handled from a central point?
- If not, what does a control model for these functions look like?

Technical

- If multiple intranets are currently active, do they share a common
  technology platform, or one that can be integrated?
- What other issues can be foreseen in achieving integration?
- What information needs to be secure and who should have access to it?

Branding

- Do divisions or units operate and maintain separate brands?
- Is the organization trying to unite under a single brand?
- From an internal perspective, what are the benefits to either maintaining separate brands or uniting under a parent brand ?

Legal

- What are the legal obstacles to consolidating or decentralizing?
- Are there any application or third-party licensing issues to resolve in consolidating or decentralizing?

Budget and Timing

- What is driving the change, and therefore the schedule?
- How will the need for the change impact the timeline?
- Where will the budget come from: Corporate, divisions and business units or a combination?

Users

3

The Key to a
Successful Intranet

The biggest single factor in the success of an intranet is its users! Organizations often don't fully understand this fact. You can spend time and effort developing an internal online environment, but if employees don't find it useful or usable, the initiative will flounder.

Users want to be productive

Employees want what the organization wants–to be productive and efficient. The intranet should be a place for a user to get in seamlessly, get the desired information and complete the task quickly and easily.

Users don't want to waste time or be frustrated by multiple logins to gain access to different parts of the site. Or search for information organized by committees and fiefdoms, not by logic. Or feel they've stepped back in time if the intranet doesn't perform to the same standards as the rest of the web.

Users' expectations are influenced by their personal experiences on the web. The speed and effectiveness of searches, pushed relevant and customized content, and access to content from a wide variety of sources all shape what users expect from their online interactions.

Most of all, users have come to expect some level of entertainment from their web experiences. Video and animations that communicate relevant information in memorable ways are one example. Podcasts and webinars that inform and educate are other tools that users have come to rely on, because they let users go at their own pace.

The advent of social media tools and capabilities has raised expectations for intranets even higher. The ability to easily and seamlessly connect to colleagues at all levels, as well as view and edit professional profiles: this is something employees will value.

The experience and interface should be centered on the user experience. Even so, there's something to be said for the familiar; the experience and interface should align with the organization and its culture. Adhering to brand standards, look and feel is one way to make the intranet experience comfortable for users.

FOCUSING ON USERS

Regardless of the state of your organization's intranet, there are four basic components you should consider before undertaking any upgrades or reinventions:

- Information architecture.

- User interface.

- Tools and functionality.

- Accessibility.

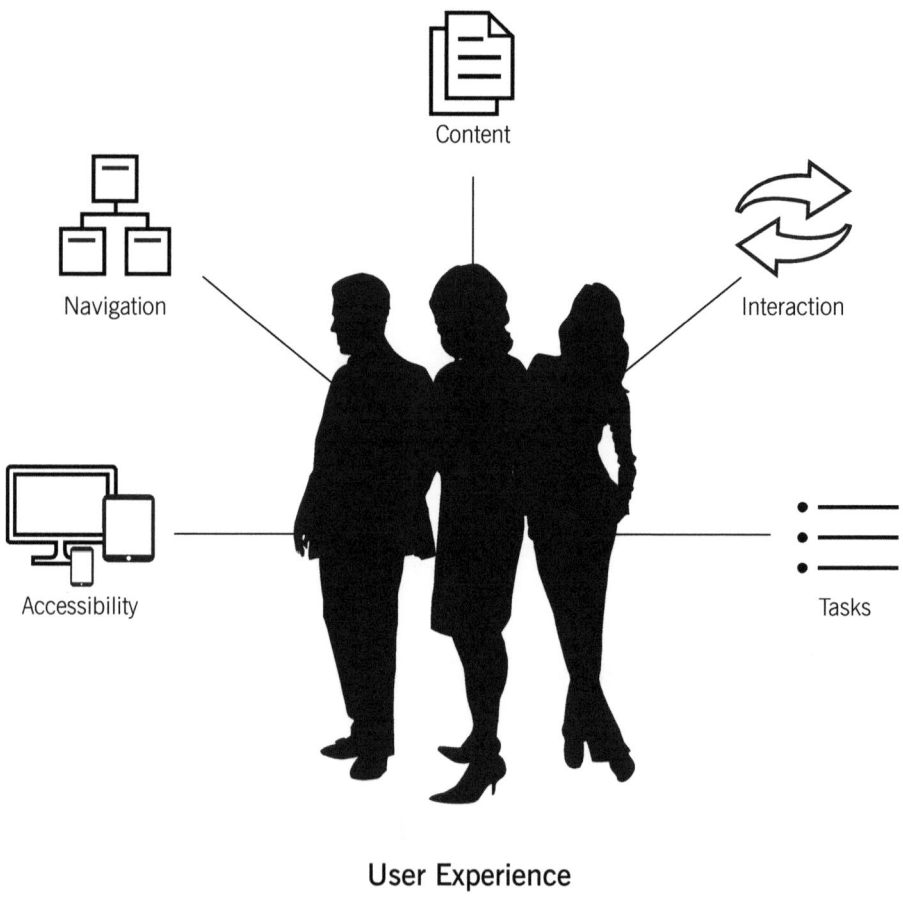

Content

Navigation

Interaction

Accessibility

Tasks

User Experience

ⓘ *Most Common Tasks Employees Complete on Their Intranet*

1. Complete a form.

2. Manage benefits.

3. Contact a colleague.

4. Find an expert.

5. Get help.

6. Request a resource – office supplies, business cards, travel arrangements, conference rooms, company computer and mobile devices, hoteling space, web and conference call reservations.

7. Do the right thing – business methodologies, project procedures, safety and quality management.

8. Stay in compliance – policies, time tracking, training requirements.

9. Track with company culture and direction.

10. Get help in an emergency.

11. Profile personal skills and role in company, participate in project teams, interest groups, and communities.

12. Interact with other employees.

Information architecture

Information architecture is the organizing of content to allow seamless access from multiple points within the online environment. Intranets are complex structures that must align user needs, business objectives and content sources.

This process begins with a thorough needs and resource analysis touching multiple sources, users, administrative functions and business units or divisions.

The most direct way to identify users' needs is to ask them. User surveys, blogs and even contests to encourage suggestions are all ways to collect relevant data.

A comprehensive understanding of the intranet's business objectives is also a critical piece in developing and aligning the information architecture for maximum effectiveness and usability. You'll want to interview or poll departmental or business unit leaders, intranet steering committees and senior management to gain a full understanding of the objectives and functions to be integrated.

The last piece of the analysis is identifying the sources of content throughout the organization (see Chapter 5). A complete inventory of current and available content needs to be catalogued and ultimately tagged for type, topic, and relevance. This becomes the starting point for creating an architecture for content.

As you analyze these components, an inventory will evolve that you can then map into an information architecture. That's what will drive the user interface.

The principles of a user interface
The user interface is about wayfinding, access and familiarity. Most of all, it's about usability.

One of the most common complaints is that users can't find what they're looking for, even when it is right in front of them. The navigation may be unclear, the design and composition of the page confusing, or content not labeled clearly or intuitively.

Applying basic user interface principles
These are issues that must be addressed. What follows is an overview of some of the basic principles of interface design broken down into three categories: navigation, page layout and color.

Navigation:

Consistent and clear navigation is the most important element of a good user interface.

- Remember the "three-click" rule: users should be able to find the basic information they need with no more than three clicks.

- Organize and label your content well. Navigation ease is critically influenced by organization and labeling. Poorly organized content requires users to navigate large "distances" to reach related pieces of information. Misleading or uninformative options and hypertext labels can send users down the wrong paths.

- Typographical solutions are recommended for navigational items; avoid using photographic images as navigational buttons.

Following are some recommendations for within-page navigation that will be relevant whether you have only a single page of content in your area or multiple pages.

- Minimize the need for horizontal scrolling. Many users avoid scrolling, so they may never see content to the left or right of what appears in the browser window.

- Across multiple pages, keep navigational elements in the same place on each page so users automatically know where to find them.

- To allow users instant, easy access to major subjects of your content area, use a navigational panel or mega-menu that displays your content subgroups. On every page of your content area, clearly indicate where your user is currently located by visually differentiating that subgroup from the others in the panel.

- Avoid the "click here" link. Instead, create links out of meaningful keywords or phrases that users will quickly see and understand.

Page Layout:
Good page layout not only optimizes user performance, but also provides a positive aesthetic experience for the user. Although aesthetic success is largely beyond the scope of this book, the following guidelines can help you with some aspects of optimizing visual performance:

- Design so users can intuitively predict where to go on the page to get information and access navigational controls.

- Establish a hierarchy for the content, then lay it out to correspond with that hierarchy.

- Present your most important information and links at the top of the page. Users tend to give up easily if they're confused or in unfamiliar territory.

- Your intranet home page should be content-driven, so never start with a splash screen that has little or no informational value.

- Avoid visual clutter from too much information, too many graphics, or too little organization.

- Group related information and give your groupings informative labels. The closer things are to each other, the more mental connections your users will make.

- It's preferable to locate your navigation elements at the top or on the left side of the screen.

Color:
Because color is perhaps the most obvious design element, choosing it requires an important set of decisions. Color has strong branding and aesthetic appeal, draws attention, and shows relationships between information.

- To help make the intranet a familiar experience for your users, be sure to choose colors specified in the organization's visual identity standards.

- Color is a powerful attention-getting tool. Use it spar-ingly, or it loses its effectiveness.

- Use colors consistently. Decide on the specific mean-ing of a color within an application and stick with it throughout.

- Although there is no standard for colors when imple-menting hypertext links, select colors for each state and stay with that system throughout the site. For instance:

  - **Blue** for an active link.
  - **Green** for a highlighted link.
  - Gray for a visited link.

You can download a complete guide to interface design from *intranetsunstuck.com.*

Tools and functionality

The third basic component in redesigning or improving your intranet is the tools and functionality that make it useful and efficient. While these will be dictated by the specifics of your business, keep two common principles in mind when planning, developing or improving the user experience.

First, the functions and the tools used to complete them must be easy to use. Second, they must be readily accessible to the user. This means more than making sure the tools are intuitive and having the intranet accessible from your home computer. Today, users expect both the functionality and accessibility they get on the company intranet to be equally present outside of work.

Accessibility

Mobile strategy, a must have

Users want easy access to the information and processes housed on the intranet: from anywhere, on any device. This means a mobile strategy for the intranet is critical. Of course there are many issues to consider. Chief among them are obtainable information and limits to what a small screen can accommodate effectively.

Security is a constant concern, and with advancements in cloud computing and remote access, many IT professionals see even more threats looming.

Currently there is no easy answer to security issues, but an intranet can't be a useful tool if it can't be accessed outside the organization's walls. Making only select information and functionality available remotely is the place to start.

The trend toward tablets may blunt the issue of limited screen size. However, the smartphone is still the ubiquitous device for most knowledge workers, so you need to take screen size into consideration. This requires a strategy for the intranet that creates a separate mobile site.

The mobile site will have to take into account limited screen real estate and limits to what can be accomplished on a mobile phone. Don't try to design the whole intranet for mobile access, just key components. Access to employee directories, time and expense inputs and reports are examples of some limited but valuable functionality that can be the basis of a mobile strategy.

Likewise, social networking tools were clearly conceived for mobile devices, so no mobile strategy can be complete without them. Adapting a social component to your mobile intranet strategy is a must if you want to take full advantage of the potential of mobile access.

Social networking has gone internal
The integration of social networking tools into all facets of an intranet can have a powerful effect on the workforce. These kinds of tools engage employees and leave them with the strong impression that their organization is innovative, collaborative, and focused on employee productivity.

Companies worldwide are discovering that such tools can help their intranets:

- Recruit, engage and retain employees.

- Empower collaboration.

- Improve business processes.

- Shorten development cycles.

- Support and reinforce the organization's brand and culture among employees.

Results like these can have real positive impact on an organization, its employees and its bottom line.

In an organizational setting, social networking tools are too often defined by a negative knee-jerk reaction to Facebook, Twitter and YouTube. However, take a closer look at the underlying concepts of these platforms and it's not hard to see how their basic functionality can engage employees and improve productivity and use of the intranet.

Three areas where social networking tools can have an impact are:

Collaboration
- Employee profile (with advanced search capabilities).
- Wikis, project spaces, blogs and microblogs, research.
- Document managing and editing tools.
- Presentation sharing.

Training
- Webcasting or live-casting.
- Video sharing.

Community
- News and information aggregation.
- Online advocacy and fundraising.
- Business reviews.

When broken down to these basic concepts, social networking tools have a place in any organization's intranet.

(i) *Steps to establishing a social networking strategy:*

1. Prioritize and align social media strategy with business objectives. Determine what you are looking to accomplish: collaboration, communication, team building, innovation, etc.

2. Determine cultural expectations – work with team leaders to establish why and how to engage with these tools.

3. Identify organizational parameters – determine the financial, cultural, legal and technical limitations to what can be done.

4. Gain senior leadership buy-in – success depends on leadership support and participation.

5. Select social tools that align to business objectives – prioritize and categorize high-level functions and choose tools that can work across categories.

6. Implement and integrate – acquire or build tools that can seamlessly integrate into your legacy systems.

7. Develop guidelines and measurement tools – establish and communicate best practices and build in measurement tools for benchmarking.

8. Benchmark, measure and improve – determine what's working and address what's not.

Some final thoughts

If focusing on users is critical to the success of an intranet, those users need a strong say in its development. Users often think they are held at the mercy of the IT department. They shouldn't be. And there's plenty your organization and your users can do about it.

Users should be driving upgrades and fixes to the intranet. They should have access to lines of communication with intranet managers and IT personnel to comment and suggest improvements. Blogs, surveys and message boards are easy and effective ways to get your users involved and keep the intranet a vital and evolving tool.

The user survey is still the best way to gain valuable insight into how the intranet is faring and what can be done to improve it. A comprehensive survey tool is available for download at intranetsunstuck.com.

Technology

4

Technology is Not the Silver Bullet

If an organization doesn't have an intranet, or has an unsuccessful one, many times the first place leadership looks for a solution is the technology market. They want to just buy an intranet, hoping that with the right tool, a good one will spontaneously happen. Technology will be their silver bullet.

Vendors of technical products feed this misguided thinking by promoting their "intranet solution" to the lucrative corporate market. Vendors who already have a presence in an organization look to the intranet space as a way to sell more tools and embed their technology more deeply. They sometimes claim that buying their tool and putting some branding on out-of-the-box templates will produce an intranet. Products of all types – content management systems, databases, portal front-ends, social media/networking tools, and search engine applications – are being sold as "intranets in a box," the "only intranet solution you will need."

Regardless of the product, technology alone won't produce a great intranet, overnight or otherwise. Often, many intranet projects initially focus too much attention on picking the right technology, scanting other important issues. They develop an RFP that addresses only IT requirements – new "industry standard" products, high-level functionality, technological fit with current technical standards and environment, technical interfaces, cost per seat, administrator and developer training needs, and, of course, ideally, some new toys and sizzle.

The effort fails to consider both organizational and employee requirements that need to be supported; integration points with other internal systems; or existing bottlenecks for employee tasks and processes. Fundamentally, this approach bows to a deeply-mistaken but long-cherished IT tenet – that if the right toolset is provided, employees will populate it, and when they don't it's the fault of the employees, not the technology.

Technology won't give you an instant intranet, because an intranet is not an idle tool, waiting for employees to use correctly if they were just savvy enough. It's not up to employees to populate and create an intranet on their own.

Successful intranets are intrinsic to organizational life, reflecting culture, brand, processes and values. They greet new employees, integrate acquisitions, facilitate day-to-day employee life, link people, offices, business groups and countries, support employees through emergencies, career and personal growth, celebrate successes and mourn losses. Technology tools on their own just sit and wait to be told what to do – a pale imitation of the real thing.

To create a successful intranet, start with understanding the full scope of requirements, and then decide which IT solution is best. You're setting up your intranet to fail if you buy the IT solution before considering user needs and integration with current systems and content.

☑ *IT Requirements Checklist*

1. Web content publishing capability supporting:
   - ☐ Distributed authorship.
   - ☐ Non-technical content managers and editors.
   - ☐ Shared information architecture, site typology, URL structure.
   - ☐ Site-wide branding and graphical interface design elements.
   - ☐ Customization to large audiences.
   - ☐ Personalization by employees.
   - ☐ Multilingual interfaces and content.
   - ☐ Site-wide management of broken links, low activity.
   - ☐ Warning, site expiration.
   - ☐ Mobile versions.
2. Employee identity management, authentication and single sign-on.
3. Integration support to connect to email and legacy systems.
4. Social networking capabilities:
   - ☐ Employee profiles.
   - ☐ Subscriptions.
   - ☐ Feedback and ratings.
   - ☐ Commenting.
   - ☐ Discussions.
   - ☐ Groups.
   - ☐ Networking, sharing, adding to network.
5. Site-wide and topic-specific search, result targeting, search request evaluation.
6. User activity analysis.

Focusing on key elements of the right technology

Single sign-on:

While they may not know the technical term, nothing captures ambivalent employees' attention to an intranet like the ability to manage their access to separate systems and reduce the number of passwords they have to deal with. Technology has advanced significantly in this area and a variety of products exist to facilitate single sign-on. Get one and implement it as broadly as possible, with user access management a prominent part of the intranet. Now.

Web content management systems:

Once implemented, the right content management system can free the intranet team from having to create and manage individual pages and documents, enabling them to focus on higher-value processes like information architecture, usability, and user experience analysis. Ultimately, an intranet's beautiful home page, simple navigation, productive search and shelf full of awards are wasted if the content can't be trusted. Giving employees easy access to insufficient content is a bad idea. Intranet teams fail when they do not take responsibility for overall content quality – even content they don't own.

Good intranet teams spend most of their time managing content, with home-grown content management systems. It should be easier than it is.

Content management on an intranet is more difficult than on a website. The volume is greater and scope broader. The intranet integrates a dispersed and disparate content manager group, and supports decentralized contribution.

At its most basic level, an intranet content management systems needs to:

- Allow for content drafting, review, approval and publishing.

- Maintain access at different levels.

- Tag every page with a date and owner.

- Manage expiration by notifying page owners that an update is needed.

- Be easy enough for a paratechnical team to manage, a nontechnical editor to use.

More sophisticated systems also:

- Separate content from design so that redesigns, branding changes, accessibility requirements and mobile versions are much easier to manage. Instead target pages, sections, and links based on an employee's attributes – geography, division, or role.

- Support link management and identify broken links.

- Allow for content to be embargoed until a defined go-live date.

- Manage taxonomy and meta-tags, including linking to search and metrics.

- Monitor regulatory and policy compliance.

- Provide automatic versioning and easy rollback.

- Incorporate reusable components, e.g., a repository or blog template, online polls/user rating functionality.

Companies with a mature intranet and the possibility of investment often find this is good time to look at web content management systems. Be warned, however, that migrating to a new CMS is a big deal, consuming considerable time and resources, and overwhelming other initiatives. It takes considerable work to move everything to a new system and just get back to what you had before. Your organization and stakeholders can't go on "hold" in the meantime.

Companies with a baby intranet ready for a bold step forward, like merging multiple intranets or doing an in-depth content audit, also find it a good time to investigate a CMS. In these cases, it may make more sense to start from scratch in the new system than attempt to migrate.

Keep in mind: While it may make the intranet team's life easier, content management is a back-end process with no direct contribution to user experience or perceived additional value to senior management. If the content isn't already being kept up to date, migrating to a new system will only give you a beautiful report on how bad things are.

ⓘ *A successful content management system*

- Contributes to content quality.
- Supports the user experience rather than defining it.
- Lightens the intranet team's load.
- Supports broad, decentralized participation.
- Helps implement taxonomy tagging and management, which will improve relevance and search.
- Stays quietly and reliably in the background, playing nicely with other technologies.
- Allows the intranet team to rest easier, not work harder.
- Supports distributing content via additional distribution channels like mobile apps.

Search:

Most intranet teams are rightly not satisfied with the quality of user search. Almost all intranets have a search engine either integrated with their content management technology or bolted on, and almost all user surveys still rank search as one of the top areas needing improvement.

The same tools that have become ubiquitous in web browsing do not deliver the same magic inside an organization. There are several reasons for this:

1. The scope and variety of intranet content is broader than public web sites' content.

2. Intranets serve as portals, linking users to stand-alone applications. Integrating search for these applications can be difficult; helping users understand what's included in site-wide search can be even more difficult.

3. Fewer people are doing the searching, so search engines have fewer patterns on which to build results.

4. Search engine optimization literature, consultants and techniques are almost exclusively focused on publicly available content, leaving intranet teams on their own to address user needs.

5. Compared to public web sites, intranets are much more likely to have "unintentional archives" of outdated content that a search engine invariably finds and ranks highly.

6. Corporate content, for legal, regulatory and other reasons, is sometimes unexpectedly named. For example, a search for "maternity leave" on many U.S. intranets should be simple, but will return no results, even though it is a key benefit. Few users think to look for it under the broader, more legally appropriate name of "Family Leave Act." The word "maternity" may never appear in the policy.

7. While internal search applications support hard-coding of "key matches," finding the right list of designated matches is difficult, and management is an ongoing problem. For example, a search for "code of conduct" should return as the top result the latest official version, not outdated versions or a question in a forum posting. Making this happen can require hard-coding. The challenge is to develop the list of the most important matches, including the terms employees use; keep it as short as possible; and make search maintenance part of regular management.

Good search on an intranet isn't an option. Despite the best navigation, user surveys regularly report that anywhere between 30%–50% of employees search before they use navigation tools.

ⓘ *Successful Search*

- Understands users' expectations that they're searching everything on the intranet, not just content controlled by the intranet team.
- Facilitates targeted and site-wide searching, e.g., the ability to search only forms, and communicates clearly to the employee which they're searching.
- Utilizes a packaged search engine users know from the Internet.
- Keeps management of index and key matches a business task, not IT's.
- Asks users for feedback after every search and regularly reviews reports for most frequently searched terms.
- Routinely makes adjustments and tracks overall success rate.
- Partners with good information architecture, doesn't attempt to cover for a bad one.
- Integrates with meta-tagging on the content management system.

Social networking tools:
Many companies are in the midst of evaluating their social media strategies. Fortunately, in most companies the effort is tied to the organization's strategy, not simply to a desire to appear youthful. The real opportunity for intranets is in leveraging the social networking technology and mindset to support the organization's relationship with employees, enhancing their sense that it knows and values them.

Emerging corporate social networking tools promise to make it significantly easier for an employee to have his or her own interaction with the intranet. These tools are even quietly solving the elusive "employee skills directory" problem, using crowdsourcing to find someone in the organization who can help with an individual's question. These features also show a lot of promise for marketing, client relationship management, recruiting and mentoring.

In order to be a benefit rather than another content or process roadblock, social networking solutions need to be flexible, supporting easy integration and evolution. You must consider business content and user interests and requirements. The best implementations integrate social media tools into the intranet structure as a single user experience.

Identifying characteristics of the wrong technology

While technology and an intranet are not the same thing, and an organization can't buy an intranet, technology can significantly enhance an intranet.

It can also kill one. Technology can do just as much damage to an intranet as out-of-date content or poor navigation, by interrupting and frustrating user processes as well as making change difficult and costly.

Most common technology mistakes:

- *The technology dictates the navigation:* the technical tool set dictates or ruins the user experience because it drives navigation in a "databasey" way rather than the way employees think.

- *Wrong development methodologies:* technical project processes designed for accounting systems (rather than agile or rapid-application processes) make intranet projects too complicated, too lengthy and too costly.

- *Too much customization:* home-grown development or too much customization of off-the-self tools prevents growth and rapid upgrade to improved functionality.

- *Poor IT support:* inadequately managed offshore or outsourced development/user support, or worse, an IT organization that does not provide support, leaves gaps in the user experience, making employees feel devalued and isolated.

- *Security concerns overshadow the user experience:* overly-enthusiastic IT security "lock-downs" and badly architected access checks make the user experience frustrating, extremely slow or generally nonproductive.

Content

Good Content is
Fundamental

5

Organizations tend to think the most challenging elements of implementing an intranet are choosing the right technology or designing an effective user experience. A common assumption is that populating the intranet with content will be the easy part.

Nothing is further from the truth. Too often there is no clear idea of:

- What content is important and relevant.

- What users prefer for accessing and using the content.

- How up-to-date or complete the current content is.

- What's involved in getting the content ready for integration into the intranet.

- How content will be maintained once the intranet is implemented.

As a result, many intranets fail because they are not delivering useful and reliable content.

A poor content strategy is one of the biggest reasons users don't find value in their intranet. Common mistakes include:

- Too little useful content is available on the intranet at launch.

- The organization is unwilling or unable to be selective about what content to include, and ends up including everything. This can occur when departments want to keep control over what content they provide or when the intranet is treated as a repository.

- Content is a hodge-podge of items based on what was available rather than on what users need.

- Content turns out to be unreliable because it is out-of-date or inaccurate, undermining users' trust in the intranet. This typically happens when content ownership is unclear.

Another challenge is maintaining content over the long run. Often, organizations put a lot of effort into cleaning up and updating their content when the intranet is first launched, but then give little thought to what's needed to keep the content fresh and relevant. Some organizations implement automated processes using meta-data that they hope will improve the relevance of content; but there is often an "automatic pilot" mentality to this, and the desired end is not achieved.

Developing or rethinking your content strategy

The Content Strategy Discussion Guide (see sidebar on page 98) is a good way to start developing or rethinking your intranet's content strategy. Developing a content roadmap is a good idea as well. The roadmap should outline the minimum needed for launch, as well as for adding, enhancing and maintaining content. Keep in mind that this roadmap should be reassessed periodically to ensure it is aligned with evolving user needs.

You can download the Content Strategy Discussion Guide from intranetsunstuck.com.

💬 Content Strategy Discussion Guide

What
- What topics?
- What forms (formats)?

Why
- Why does this provide business value?
- Why will employees care?

How
- How will content needs be identified?
- How will the content be developed?
- How will the content be delivered?
- How will the content be maintained?
- How will the content be measured?

Where
- Where will we get the content?

When
- When will the content be published?
- When will the content be updated?
- When will it be expired/decomissioned?

Who
- Who is responsible for creating the content?
- Who is responsible for publishing and producing the content?
- Who is responsible for updating the content?

Also, it is important to think about what should be trimmed or eliminated. Content strategy is not just deciding what you're going to include. It's also deciding what you're going to leave out.

An intranet can cover a wide range of content types. Deciding on content categories and the specific content to be included in each requires careful analysis and balancing of user needs, corporate culture and communications goals.

(i) *Typical Intranet Categories:*

- Our organization.
- News and communications.
- Our people.
- Human Resources.
- Training and career development.
- Knowledge and research.
- Marketing and sales.
- Policies and related forms.
- Department and administrative tasks.
- Project and project resources.
- Employee group or communities.

See the Typical Intranet Content Categories listing with content examples on the next four pages. The tool is also available for download at intranetsunstuck.com.

☑ Typical Intranet Content Categories

Content Category	Content Examples
Our Organization	☐ Mission Statement ☐ Company History ☐ Annual Report ☐ Awards and Industry Rankings ☐ Investor Relationships ☐ Leadership Team ☐ Organizational Structure ☐ Org Charts ☐ Priorities and Values
News and Communications	☐ Company News, Earnings Announcements, Awards ☐ Quarterly Activity Report ☐ Emergency Announcements, Procedures, Employee Assistance ☐ Departmental Announcements ☐ Employee Achievements and Obituaries ☐ Company Community Involvement ☐ Company Press Releases ☐ Competitor or Market News ☐ Newsletters
Our People	☐ Directories ☐ Leadership Profiles ☐ Employee Profiles ☐ Volunteer/Community ☐ Opportunities

Projects and Project Resources

- [ ] Signature Projects
- [ ] Project Profiles
- [ ] Project Management
- [ ] Project Team Sites
- [ ] Project Services
- [ ] Health and Safety Standards
- [ ] Quality Standards

Policies and Forms

- [ ] Ethical Standards
- [ ] Code of Conduct
- [ ] Policies
- [ ] Procedures and Methodologies
- [ ] Forms

Knowledge and Research

- [ ] Third-Party Research Sources

Administrative Tasks and Departmental Information

- [ ] Time and Expense
- [ ] IT Procurement, Support, Security, Projects
- [ ] Meeting Room Reservations
- [ ] Travel Reservations and Management
- [ ] Procurement
- [ ] Legal
- [ ] Contracts Management and Compliance
- [ ] International Guidance/Export Controls
- [ ] Finance and Accounting

☑ Typical Intranet Content Categories / continued

Content Category	Content Examples
Human Resources	☐ Employee Benefit Packages and Self-Service Tools ☐ Benefit Providers ☐ Employee Assistance Program ☐ Employee Discounts ☐ Employee Stock Purchase Plan ☐ Holiday Schedule ☐ HR Policies and Forms ☐ New Employees ☐ Retirement Plans ☐ Vacation and Leave Policies ☐ Recruiting ☐ Referral and Transfers ☐ Veterans ☐ Staffing - Temporary, Subcontractors
Marketing and Sales	☐ Awards ☐ Boilerplate ☐ Business Development ☐ Branding and Templates ☐ Brochures ☐ Capabilities ☐ Client Accounts ☐ Collateral Materials ☐ Company Store ☐ Company Facts and Description ☐ Customer Lists ☐ Lead Tracking

	☐ Maps
	☐ Presentations
	☐ Proposals and Proposal Tracking
	☐ Resumes/CVs
	☐ Rankings
	☐ Services
	☐ SOQs
	☐ Target Lists
Training and Career Development	☐ Company Training Requirements
	☐ Employee Training Status Tracking
	☐ Training Opportunities and Learning Management Systems
	☐ Educational Benefits
Employee Groups/ Communities	☐ Innovation/Joint Research
	☐ Business Line Sites
	☐ Operating Group Sites
	☐ Team Sites
	☐ Project Sites
	☐ Local Office Sites
	☐ Practice Groups
	☐ Communities of Interest
	☐ Discussion Threads
	☐ Restricted Departmental Sites
	☐ Personal Employee Circles

Managing content as you move forward

Effective content management is not simple. It requires careful planning, well-thought-out processes, standards, discipline, and most importantly, diligence. You must focus on ensuring that all content on the intranet is reliable and trustworthy. That means there need to be processes for maintaining what's already there as well as standards for adding and retiring content.

Content ownership is a key element in good content management. All content on the intranet needs to have an identified owner, and ownership responsibilities need to be clearly spelled out. Often, owners want to focus on where and how the content is displayed rather than on more mundane content maintenance processes. Keeping owners focused on content quality is one of the more important responsibilities of the intranet manager, and should always be a priority.

A good content management system can be very helpful for monitoring content freshness and quality. You'll want to establish and monitor taxonomy and tagging standards for each type of content. You can set parameters for content freshness and expiration, with the system notifying owners of the need for updates, or for verification that the content is still valid. Links can be checked to ensure that they work correctly.

Also, your search functionality will benefit significantly from strong content management standards and processes. If your intranet includes content from third parties, it's also important to make sure copyrights and terms of use for this content are understood and implemented properly.

(i) Taxonomy Tips

Taxonomy development at an organization-wide level is a challenge, but it can be met. The KISS principle applies – do enough but don't attempt to be absolutely comprehensive, either in the taxonomy itself or in its application.

- Good indexing and a well-structured taxonomy are essential for search accuracy and relevance.
- While technology is key to taxonomy management, don't underestimate the value of human intervention. Effective taxonomy management requires the skills of information scientists and librarians. A blended approach of people plus technology will yield the best results.
- Avoid too much complexity in the taxonomy, and recognize that it will require continued maintenance.
- Apply the taxonomy only to content that is worth indexing and searching for.

Content value via social networking tools

While social networking tools aren't what we commonly think of when we think of content, they can be an important part of your content strategy, helping employees:

- Find each other and make connections.

- Network and share with each other.

- Facilitate group collaboration.

These tools help companies nurture corporate culture and stay connected with employees. They can also stimulate awareness of the intranet and help employees discover what else is there.

But like everything else planned for the intranet, social networking needs a purpose. Start with defining clear objectives for how social networking tools will support business objectives and nurture *esprit de corps*.

When content consolidation is required

If you're consolidating content from recently acquired businesses or previously existing intranets, developing a strategy for integrating this content will be a significant challenge. Typically, there'll be varying degrees of content quality, as well as overlap and duplication.
In addition, there could be content ownership conflicts and other sensitive political issues you'll need to work

through carefully. In the end, though, meeting user needs and creating a consistent and aligned user experience must be first priorities and should drive consolidation strategy.

Regardless of the amount of content to be consolidated, it's critical to perform a content assessment and develop a content consolidation plan. The Content Consolidation Steps diagram on the next page shows the steps to ensure that all content to be integrated has been reviewed. This approach will also help you navigate and negotiate through any ownership or political sensitivities. In some cases you may want to bring in a third party who can offer an independent perspective on the decisions you need to make.

Content should be assessed for quality, duplication and uniqueness. Contractual agreements and data confidentiality rules also need to be reviewed and included in the assessment. Some tough decisions will need to be made about what stays, what goes and how content will be integrated. The consolidation plan should address how the content will be categorized and aligned into an integrated content structure.

Once you've developed a strawman of the new content structure, vet it with content owners and stakeholders to reach a consensus. If possible, the consolidation approach should be piloted and refined based on feedback before full implementation.

A more detailed Content Consolidation Roadmap is available for download at intranetsunstuck.com.

Content Consolidation Steps

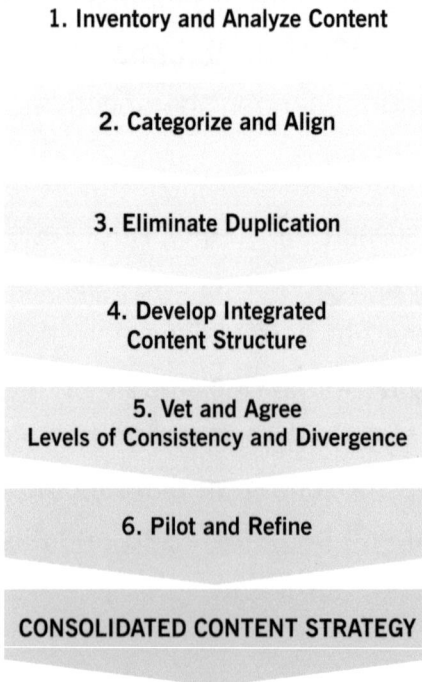

1. Inventory and Analyze Content

2. Categorize and Align

3. Eliminate Duplication

4. Develop Integrated
Content Structure

5. Vet and Agree
Levels of Consistency and Divergence

6. Pilot and Refine

CONSOLIDATED CONTENT STRATEGY

ⓘ Content-based Approach to Consolidation of Departmental, Divisional or Competing Intranets

1. Identify an experienced, unbiased third-party resource.

2. Conduct a simple but detailed analysis of all existing target content, noting content groupings, navigational paths, and if possible, scope and ownership of content.

3. Based on major content "chunks," align the content from the various intranets into rough categories, then review content in major categories to identify where it is exactly the same, similar, or truly unique.

4. Develop a strawman high-level shared content structure covering all major content areas, and ask each intranet team to map their content to the new structure to identify issues and gaps.

5. Agree levels of consistency, targeting, and divergence.

6. Pilot and refine.

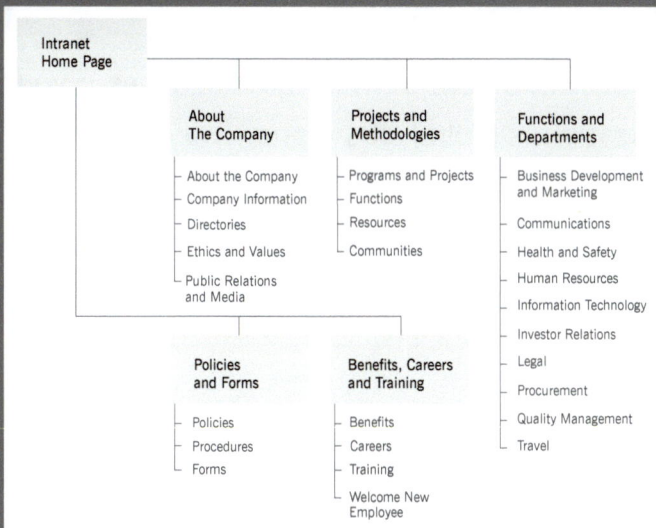

Some final thoughts on content

In conclusion, as you work on making sure your intranet has content employees find valuable and use regularly, remember:

- Content is most effectively managed by the departments that own it.

- Content should be clearly marked with an identified owner and the most recent update date.

- Don't underestimate the editorial commitment needed to keep content fresh and relevant.

- User needs should be monitored – both what's being used and what additions are being requested.

- Content is more than text. It can come in many forms, and its form and format need to keep pace with what users expect.

- Think about content in multiple languages if your organization is global. It's a great way to demonstrate that users come first.

ⓘ *Translating Content: What's the Best Approach?*

You don't need to get carried away – focus on translating global or enterprise-wide content that will have the broadest appeal.
Examples:
- Key strategic messages.
- "Feel good" content that nurtures corporate culture.
- Code of conduct.
- Global policies.
- Mandatory employee notifications.
- Marketing and sales information used with customers.

Translate only what you can maintain and keep up to date over the long run.

Leave local content in the local language. It's not necessary to translate everything into English, and if the translation is poor, there is the added risk of misunderstanding or misinterpretation.

Resources

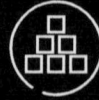

The Right Resources

6

Every intranet team will say they are underresourced, and be right. No intranet team ever has enough resources. As an "overhead" project in the corporate structure, they inevitably make do with less than the ideal. But with a good strategy and a way to set priorities, they can be very effective. A significantly underresourced intranet, however, or one with the wrong team, is destined to fail.

Establishing leadership requirements and roles

In a successful intranet, the team is led by a sponsor/champion who has a direct relationship with senior management and the leadership team. The leader needs to see the big picture, have credibility with leadership, and report to senior management.

The leader drives strategy and sets the pace, keeping the intranet closely aligned with business strategy and priorities. He or she is a passionate employee advocate, whose dedication to doing right by the user is the deciding factor when groups or priorities conflict. The leader doesn't see himself/herself as saddled with an additional responsibility on top of existing duties, but as someone whose job would not exist without the intranet.

The importance of the leader role should not be under-estimated. Many intranets are buried in obscurity in organizations where anybody can say no, but nobody can say yes. The intranet leader is the person who can and will make decisions and stick with them through implementation.

This individual should be the chair of the steering group/governance body, ensuring cross-functional participation and representation; however, the leader should also maintain a high level of interaction with the intranet working team.

Creating a dedicated cross-functional team

Successful intranets are managed by a dedicated team who coordinate technical functionality, navigation, design and content across the organization. The core team usually sits in the unit with the largest stake in the intranet, such as Corporate Communications, with direct links to other key stakeholders such as Human Resources, Information Technology, or Knowledge Management.

The team is practical and thrifty, with a balance of project-oriented and operational personalities. They are comfortable with but unimpressed by technologists, and work easily in the space between technology, content and business.

Third-party/vendor management skills are increasingly important as internal processes are outsourced and web services like search and metrics use third-party packages.

Following is an overview of key non-IT roles for an intranet team. These aren't all necessarily full time equivalent positions, or all in the same organizational unit, or even all employees. While it's common to think an intranet team needs to be in one organizational unit, that is not necessarily true. An intranet team can be created and successful in several ways: 1) as a single organizational unit, 2) as a core team supplemented by part-time staff from elsewhere in the organization, and 3) as a core team augmented by contractors. Detailed job descriptions are available for download at intranetsunstuck.com.

Intranet Manager

Home Page Editor

Producer or
Client Manager

At a bare minimum, a successful intranet has the following:

The Intranet Manager is responsible for leading the initiative and driving the strategic priorities related to its successful implementation and utilization. He/she is accountable for defining and meeting project goals, and ensuring that they are aligned with business priorities. He/she oversees the complex processes that ensure continued quality as well as buy-in from stakeholders. He/she leads the effort to identify needs, define requirements, redesign business processes, and plan projects. Ultimately the manager is responsible for defining and maintaining relationships with IT, the steering group, vendors and internal stakeholders, and ensuring progress toward organizational priorities while improving the end-user experience.

Producers or **Client Managers** are well-organized paratechnical project managers with momentum. Their job is to identify stakeholder needs, develop and manage a site from conception to successful integration, and effectively communicate the value of the offering. This is a hands-on position requiring consultative skills as well as the ability to problem-solve, and to manage and expedite production-oriented processes. These are not "check the box" project managers; they take a new functionality or application and move it from conception through all the stakeholders and steps to becoming a useful resource.

The Home Page Editor finds, attracts, writes, edits and coordinates news for freshness, accuracy, appropriateness and consistency with corporate communications strategy. He/she ensures there is always a "there" there, making the intranet personal and local.

An **intranet dream team** would include all the foregoing slots plus the following additional roles (in black):

User Experience
Specialist

Intranet Manager

Human Resources
Specialist

Home Page Editor

Policy Person

Producer or
Client Manager

Social Networking
Specialist

Company Information
Specialist

Search Optimization
Specialist

Metrics and
Analytics Specialist

Change Manager

Quality Assurance
Manager

User Experience Specialist. This position develops usability/user experience strategy. He/she is responsible for ensuring the intranet meets industry standards for usability, conforms to government standards for accessibility and adheres to brand standards. This individual possesses deep expertise in usability and accessibility standards, as well as branding guidelines and the content integration process. He/she proactively identifies issues and complexities of usability and takes the lead on prototyping and testing new applications and navigational models. Responsibilities also include monitoring and responding to user feedback and questions, and educating the larger team on issues and user patterns.

Human Resources Specialist. Benefits are complicated, timeframes are short, and employees must respond or lose out, leaving the employee at risk and the organization circling noncompliance. Internet technology has changed Human Resources perhaps more than any other part of the corporation. HR depends on the intranet. It's critical to have a team member focused on supporting HR messages and resources.

Policy Person. Every successful major organization has its Policy Person. This stereotypically socially-challenged gem of a resource lives and breathes corporate policy and procedure, and takes personally every word, style and format change. He/she knows how the policies interrelate and vary by geography, exactly what needs to be updated with major corporate events, and which translation vendors can be trusted with corporate codicils. More often a legal department employee than an official part of the intranet team, the Policy Person cares for her/his area of the intranet like a doting granny. Finding change difficult, the PP may need special attention and probably extra oxygen during redesigns and system migrations.

Social Networking Specialist. Social networking should be part of the organization's business and communications strategy and integral to overall intranet strategy. A key element in its integration is the inclusion of a social media specialist as part of the intranet team. This position manages whatever social networking tools are used, as well as monitoring online community activities – nurturing them, making sure nothing inappropriate is posted, making sure questions are answered and ensuring that social networking activity is healthy, robust and aligned with overall strategy. This role also helps integrate social networking tools into communications processes.

Company Information Specialist. She or he stays awake at night if the latest management changes are not posted or employee totals not updated. This role doesn't just coordinate, but owns, the most important corporate content – directories, organizational charts, quarterly results and the like.

Search Optimization Specialist. This specialist is responsible for optimizing the search experience on the intranet. He/she monitors search usage to identify problems and opportunities for improvement. The position defines and manages taxonomy, topic sets, synonym lists and other content management-related tasks that have an impact on the search experience. The SO specialist has significant interaction with key content owners and manages search projects.

Metrics and Analytics Specialist. This team member will manage gathering, analyzing and reporting on usage levels and patterns. This includes working with stakeholders to understand their measurement needs and developing approaches, reports and processes to meet them. He/she is also responsible for compiling and analyzing regular monthly and quarterly reports as well as ad-hoc reports. He/she manages prioritizing report requests and ensuring that they are delivered on-time. This role is also responsible for analyzing metrics, including under-utilized content and sites, to gain a deeper understanding of usage patterns and identify opportunities for improvement. In addition, he/she manages the quality assurance process for metrics, identifying content that is not tracked, and works with the appropriate resources to resolve issues.

Change Manager. This manager works across all constituencies of the intranet to ensure that communication, stakeholder management, leadership alignment, training and behavior issues are addressed. He/she ensures content, process and business management initiatives focus on enhancing the user experience and improving usababilty. The Change Manager is responsible for creating awareness and understanding throughout the organization, and promoting employee readiness for effective intranet usage.

Quality Assurance Manager. This team member works with stakeholders to ensure the overall quality of the intranet experience. He/she possesses a detailed knowledge of online best practices, content and brand standards, e-risk issues, organization and intranet strategy, house style, user experience and search engine optimization strategy. He/she is focused on delivering a consistently high-quality user experience for all empoyees and a high level of stakeholder satistfaction.

Choosing an organizational structure: centralized versus decentralized

Some intranet teams are highly centralized within an organization, while others are spread across divisions and geographies. There is no right structure; the team's organization should reflect the business organization, with content ownership/management and compliance decentralized so that those roles are as close to the employee as possible.

Generally speaking, if there is a choice, it's usually most productive to have the dream team centralized, coordinating its specialties with their counterparts in different divisions, departments, and geographies. However, if it is centralized, it is important to have both formal and informal structures in place to link the team with the rest of the organization. If the intranet team is too siloed, it won't be effective.

Partnering with third-party resources

Many intranet teams incorporate third-party resources into their major initiatives and ongoing efforts. These experts help a team quickly modulate for redesigns, migrations, and the implementation of new applications, functionality or technical tools. Companies most frequently partner with third-party resources for strategy development, content analysis and design, particularly in the case of mergers and acquisitions, graphical user and user experience design, migration, and project management of major initiatives. The successful intranet manager develops a cadre of trusted partners who can be quickly integrated into the intranet team for maximum benefit.

The most productive third-party intranet resources:

- Have a long-term relationship with the intranet team.

- Are small companies, flexible and creative.

- Are local to the intranet, its team, and the organization the intranet is serving. They don't have their own agenda or tools they are looking to sell.

- Have in place ongoing service agreements that can quickly be the basis for spinning up statements of work.

7

Communications

*The Intranet is Often
an Organization's
Best Kept Secret*

Change can be difficult for any organization. When it comes to an intranet, it can be paralyzing. Communicating that change can help.

It takes an enormous effort from all involved to get an intranet off the ground or reinvented. To realize a return on an intranet investment, organizations need to communicate effectively. Communications can do more than inform: they can build awareness and acceptance for a new or redesigned intranet. A well-thought-out communications strategy can do more than prepare users for change; it can build excitement and anticipation.

The communications strategy should take a multilevel approach. Its two main phases are pre- and post-launch. Within both phases there are multiple audiences that will need information – making an integrated communications plan essential.

PRE-LAUNCH COMMUNICATIONS

Pre-launch communications have three objectives:

- To provide timely information and progress updates to the intranet team as well as stakeholders and sponsors.

- To direct and encourage word-of-mouth communication from a select group of early adopters and testers.

- To announce what changes are coming and how they will benefit all employees.

Communicating beyond the core team

Keeping the intranet team, stakeholders, and sponsors informed is a task whose importance increases directly with the size of an organization. Each stakeholder or manager will need to know about all the additions or enhancements planned for the intranet, as well as about progress, delays and issues.

For instance, Human Resources won't necessarily know what kind of collaboration the business units have planned, or what marketing materials are being posted for easy organization-wide download. Keeping all stakeholders informed – steering committees, department heads, business units, IT and most importantly, content providers – will be critically important as the initiative moves forward.

ⓘ Communication Plan Outline

Pre-Launch Communications

12 months out

Intranet team and stakeholders – communicate progress, changes.

4-6 months out

Intranet evangelists – test user groups that provide feedback and communicates buzz through word of mouth.

4-6 weeks out

All users – communicate what's coming and why.

Post-Launch

Ongoing

Intranet team, content managers and stakeholders – communicate updates, changes.

Ongoing

All users – communicate updates, changes.

Creating buzz through beta-testing

Communications to employees and stakeholders can take many forms besides traditional promotional campaigns. An interesting way to prepare employees for what's coming might be asking a select number of users to be beta-testers. This serves the purpose of gaining additional insight into the effectiveness and usability of the intranet, but will also go a long way to build word of mouth about the changes afoot.

The beta-testers should be key influencers in their departments or units. Choose people who lead teams or are outspoken within their work groups. Once this group has provided feedback, it's critical to address their concerns in order to maintain credibility. After you've done that, encourage the beta-testers to spread their thoughts and excitement within their teams and departments to create buzz.

Communicate why, not just what

Users should be made aware of what's coming, what's changing and when. Most critically, they need to understand how they will benefit from the changes. Otherwise adoption will be a struggle.

Leading up to the launch of your intranet, there should be a comprehensive communications push to alert employees to what is coming. In many cases, organizations don't think about this until it's too late for the communications to have a positive impact on the launch. It's assumed that announcing the day of the launch will be enough, or that employees will already know about the new intranet or discover the upgrades on their own. This can lead to employees' being surprised by changes, and this often starts things off on the wrong foot.

In this stage of the strategy, we recommend communicating a plan to all employees four to six weeks prior to launch. This plan should include multiple scheduled communication events leading up to the launch. Again, the key is to tell *why* the intranet is changing and what it means for the user.

Types of communications include:

- Highlights of key features or enhancements, including new functionality and how it will improve user productivity.

- Information about an organizational and/or intranet rebranding.

- Explanation of any consolidation of divisions or acquisitions.

While the key objective of the communications campaign is to inform, it should also build excitement and anticipation. The approach should be creative and promotional—creating momentum for the intranet as well as raising employee expectations.

☑ Communications Planning Checklist

When developing a communications plan, each event should:

- ☐ Identify specific audience or audiences.
- ☐ Specify media or method to be employed.
- ☐ Define the purpose of the communication.
- ☐ List key messages to be included in each communication.
- ☐ Schedule timing of events from beginning to delivery.

POST-LAUNCH COMMUNICATIONS

Communications don't end at launch. They help engage users during the early stages of an intranet's introduction or relaunch, and are essential to keeping them aware of improvements and changes. You'll need a comprehensive plan to facilitate the messaging and timing of communications going forward.

Ongoing communications

The intranet can be the most powerful communications tool available – so leverage it. It gives you a platform for posting news items, upgrade alerts and announcements of corporate-wide events that can take place on the intranet, such as photo contests and the like.

Enlist the intranet's content providers, editors and managers in both developing the communications plan and implementing it. They can be a great asset in identifying communications opportunities.

Ongoing communications will go a long way to engage users and promote full adoption of your intranet.

Social communications

Social networking is not a new tactic in communications strategies, but there's still a lot of room to experiment in an internal campaign. For instance, sending tweets or other forms of short messages to promote upgrades, surveys and contests is one way to communicate about the intranet; posting developments or updates on the organization's Facebook or LinkedIn page is another.

In addition, users can use social tools to help communicate the advantages of the intranet, as well as point out areas that need improvement. The ability to like, rate and comment on articles, features and other components can yield valuable feedback.

Of course, you need to structure and manage this interaction appropriately. Soliciting relevant, timely and honest feedback that can be shared throughout the organization will help make the intranet an ever-improving tool.

Training sessions as communications

Much like beta-testing, post-launch training sessions can have a similar result but on a larger scale. Giving employees demonstrations or training sessions highlighting intranet features and the best ways to use them will not only increase intranet activity, but also expand word-of-mouth communications about the benefits of the intranet. Nothing builds user interest and confidence better than hearing about the features from a peer or colleague.

You can handle demonstrations in several ways. For example, you can schedule in-person sessions at specific locations throughout the organization or offer webinars that can be logged into at designated times. Or you can develop downloadable tutorials that give users a sense of familiarity and comfort with the intranet but let them listen at their own pace.

A complete Communications Plan outline is available at intranetsunstuck.com, where you can download the tool as a template.

Measurement

8

How Do You Know Your Intranet Is Successful?

Assessing the progress and success of your intranet should be an integral component of management strategy. The challenge for many organizations is determining what to measure, what the metrics mean, and what to do next. It's critical to link measurement to value, be it time-saving, revenue generation, or faster onboarding of new employees. We'd recommend using both quantitative and qualitative measures and tying these to regular assessment and planning process.

Monitor and measure

With the growing sophistication of metric analytics software, it's relatively easy to create a variety of metrics to monitor and track intranet activity. But keeping reporting simple is not so easy, and sometimes the volume of data can be overwhelming and difficult to interpret.

There are four areas of measurement to focus on:

- *User activity* – usage levels as well as traffic patterns.

- *Content activity* – including social networking activity – what is popular, what's getting little traffic.

- *User feedback* – both what comes in through a help desk or Contact Us and proactive outreach to users via surveys and focus groups.

- *Systems activity* – performance as well as information about peak times and average transaction times.

By looking at these four areas together, you can get a good sense of current activity, what's working and what needs improvement.

How to measure intranet success

User Activity	Content Activity	User Feedback	Systems Activity
Unique visitors	Page visits	Help desk logs	Speed and performance indicators
Unique logins per day	Content ratings and favorites	Online user surveys	Peak times
Visits	Social networking (employee profiles created; number of comments)	Focus groups	Time per transaction
Traffic patterns			Bandwidth use
Top 10 tasks			Devices used
Activity trends	Content tagged for personal collections		
Activity of champions and trend-setters	Search results		
	Search queries		
	Lack of activity		

It's also important to rate how the intranet is doing from a strategic perspective. Some questions to answer are:

- Is the intranet's brand recognized by employees?
- Is the intranet referenced in company communications?
- How embedded is the intranet in the company's culture?
- How engaged and interested are employees?

Keep business context in mind
It's important to look at the intranet in the context of the larger business environment. It can't help productivity much if business processes remain off-line, or if salespeople on the road can't access it. The coverage of the intranet, in terms of business units, geography, and various teams, obviously has implications for its impact.

Assess and take action

Collecting metrics and user feedback is the best way to understand current levels and types of activity. It's an essential part of ongoing management. However, the metrics data, along with other types of assessments, should also be used as you step back periodically and take a holistic view of progress against strategy. This can help you fine-tune your strategy–few strategies are perfectly on target from the start.

Or, it may just not be working, and a rethinking of the entire approach is needed. It's better to know that sooner rather than later.

The Annual Intranet Assessment Checklist outlined in the next two pages provides an easy-to-use framework for a regular assessment of your intranet strategy. The critical first step is to define your intranet's goals in three main categories:

- Strategic intent – questions that provide strategic context for the intranet.

- Intranet specifics – the details of your strategy.

- Foundation for the future – key considerations for ensuring the long-term health of the intranet.

Defining goals will take some thought, but once you've done it, it's easy to assess progress against goals on a regular basis. Using this exercise as a base, you can think through implications for ongoing activities or next year's plan, and identify next steps. These next steps should be prioritized and planned. The point is to keep thinking about what you want to achieve, to be honest about progress, and then to tie that knowledge to action.

Download the Annual Intranet Assessment Framework from
intranetsunstuck.com

☑ Annual Intranet Assessment Framework

	What are stated goals?
Strategic Intent	
Reaching target groups	
Communicating corporate culture	
Supporting business priorities	
Intranet Specifics	
Compelling user experience	
Information architecture	
Visual identity	
Consolidation and integration	
Internal content	
Third-party content	
Search	
Community/social media	
Measurement and analytics	
Performance and reliability	
Communications and support	
Foundation for the Future	
Stakeholder ownership	
Resources	
Funding	
Monitoring of user needs	
Agility and flexibility to innovate	
Technology maintainability and enhancement	
Quality assurance processes	

What progress has been made?	What are implications and recommended actions?

9

Improvement

Launch is Only the Beginning

Many organizations focus a great deal of attention and investment on getting their corporate intranet built and launched. Then, once it's launched, their attention and commitment dissipate and they move on to the next big thing. They underestimate the level of effort needed to keep an intranet dynamic and alive. They don't understand or plan for:

- What it takes to adequately maintain their intranet, in particular the content and tools it makes available.

- The evolution of technology.

- The impact of corporate events like acquisitions and spinoffs.

- The changing needs of employees.

Sometimes, there's a false belief that once the intranet is launched, keeping it up to date can be automated, or put on "auto-pilot"; and while it's true that automated processes can help with maintenance, totally relying on this approach is unrealistic.

Managing post-launch

Launch is only the beginning. Post-launch, the intranet manager must ensure that the strategy and its benefits remain clear to each stakeholder group. Leadership of these stakeholder groups will change, as will the owners of the content and applications. A continuous dialogue is needed to ensure that new stakeholders and content owners understand the intranet strategy and its context.

Effective intranet management also requires standardized processes and rules. Once they're in place, the challenge will be to achieve and maintain widespread compliance. It is critical for not only the processes and rules, but also the rationale and benefits of compliance, to be well explained and communicated. Also, the easier it is to comply, the higher the levels of compliance will be. You'll need sustained communications explaining processes and rules, and these topics should be addressed in ongoing management plans.

The intranet manager can't do this alone. He/she must have buy-in from key stakeholder groups. They must have a sense of ownership.

Maintaining a relevant, high-quality and dynamic intranet must be seen as a joint responsibility, or it will become increasingly difficult to get the support to maintain a successful intranet over the long run.

ⓘ *Principles for Ongoing Intranet Improvement*

Context	Make strategy and benefits clear to each stakeholder group.
Clarity	Explain rules and processes, and highlight the benefits of compliance.
Easy	Make compliance with rules easy by providing guidance, training and support.
Sustained	Maintain communications and support over an extended period.
Ownership	Ensure that key stakeholder groups have "skin in the game."

Staying relevant and agile

Once an intranet has been launched, the next challenge is putting in place the building blocks that will help keep it relevant to both employees and the business.

A successful intranet is dynamic and must continue to evolve. Continuous improvement can take many forms. Small, incremental improvements in response to user feedback can yield major payback in user satisfaction and usage levels. More significant changes because of evolving business needs or technology trends may require more planning and budget, but if the principle of continuous improvement is baked into the annual budgeting and planning process right from the start, you should be able to address these improvements effectively.

A commitment to continuous improvement acknowledged by the business sponsor and leadership will make it significantly easier to respond to changing user needs and technology evolution. *Don't let this slip – it's critical.*

Also, a small but important point: chances are you didn't get to implement everything desired or planned for the initial launch. Don't forget about these items. Incorporate them into future plans.

Staying relevant and agile means you must:

- Be relentless about understanding what your users need. Keep asking your employees for feedback – what they like and don't like. Never forget that their needs will continue to change, and the intranet will need to change along with those needs.

- Assume technological change will impact the users' expectations. In the 21st century, technology change is the constant. Plan for it.

- Stay aligned with business priorities. As important

as keeping users satisfied is staying relevant to the business. A key element of intranet management is ensuring that the intranet strategy is aligned with business priorities, not just in the first year but in every year after that.

- Remain open to new ideas. Innovation is the lifeblood of a successful intranet.

If your intranet hasn't met expectations, don't panic. Continuous improvement principles can apply in this situation too. You probably don't need to re-launch, absent a significant business reason. A more effective approach may be to get the most critical changes implemented, and then keep making improvements. Supported by a strong communications effort, this approach can get users to try again and change their minds about the intranet's benefits.

Building blocks for the future

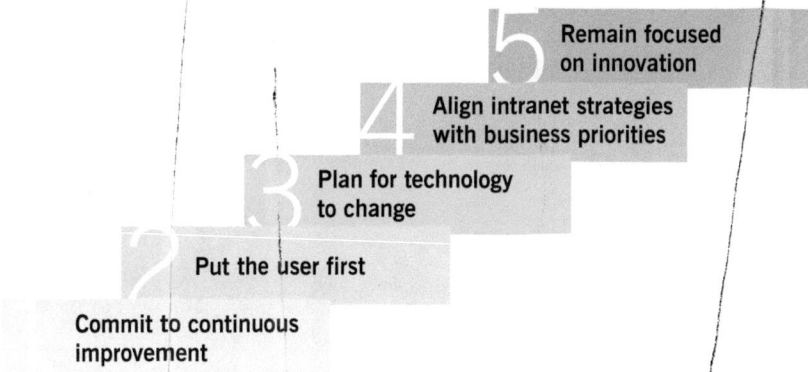

5 Remain focused on innovation

4 Align intranet strategies with business priorities

3 Plan for technology to change

2 Put the user first

Commit to continuous improvement

Conclusion

10

What makes
an Intranet Great

Intranets get stuck and fail to reach their full potential for a lot of reasons. They're always in process, constantly reinventing themselves to track with organizational changes, technology developments, and employee needs and expectations.

Successful intranets share five key characteristics.

A great intranet has a company-wide mission
The organization has only one intranet and it is officially recognized. It supports business strategy and leads corporate change. Senior management knows it, uses it, and has requirements for it. It is strategic, planned, and cost-effective, and has a clearly defined owner. It coordinates all major functions and has a broad base of stakeholders. It is integrated with other corporate systems such as email, and is governed by standards and policies.

The day a brand change is effective, the intranet announces it and reflects only the new brand. When divisional names are changed, the new names are introduced and in use throughout the intranet. Acquisitions and mergers are announced and their employees and content integrated.

A great intranet has a real home page

Successful intranets have a real home page that is a destination in itself. The home page is active, attractive, full of photos and all about the company and its employees. It demonstrates the brand and provides a sense of the company and its values. Public companies have a live stock quote, international ones have a world clock customized to their major locations.

There are stories about corporate wins, organizational changes, new initiatives and company leadership. Other stories highlight employee achievements, project awards, newly published papers, new joiners, and employee obituaries. Some include a live feed of published news about the company, its competitors and clients. Some have "After Hours" sections covering office sports teams, blood donation drives and employee time invested in charitable initiatives. Every segment allows employees to contribute ideas, articles and photos.

Great home pages also orient employees and get them quickly to what they need. Most have a section for Favorites or Frequently Used Resources – one-click access to time sheets, travel reservations, benefits, and the like.

The home page also provides consistent access to site-wide functions such as search, single sign-on and the basic organization of the content, via tabs or other navigational devices.

In one recent user-pattern study the organization learned that thirty percent of employees visit the home page and stay there. Forty percent visit the home page and then click through to major resources. Twenty percent visit the home page and then conduct a search. Only ten percent drill down to the second-level content via the tabs.

The home page is crucial – if there's no "there" there, there'll be no employees there either.

A great intranet has balanced, trusted content

When employees need a specific piece of content, that information needs to be accurate, trustworthy and easy to find. The policy sought needs to be complete, the per-diem rates the latest, the form the appropriate one for the user's geography or business unit.

Many company-wide intranets had their start in a single department (probably Human Resources or Knowledge Management), and they tend to be heavy in that type of content and lacking in other key areas. Successful intranets have a critical mass of the full scope of content employees need, organized for the employee, not the organization.

A great intranet is where the organization meets employees, and employees meet each other

The main difference between an intranet and a web site is that the intranet puts an official face on an organization. A great one uses smart design, good content, and shared structure to bring all the facets of an organization into a cohesive, manageable whole that is approachable and welcoming. Well-integrated social networking features allow employees to introduce themselves to the company, find friends and resources, and stay connected across geographies and practice groups.

A great intranet keeps up with user needs and expectations

User needs, technology and usability strategies keep evolving, and a successful intranet keeps pace. A good intranet doesn't need to be cutting-edge in technology enhancements, but it does need to be dynamic, able to change and committed to innovation and continuous improvement.

In conclusion, if you have a great intranet, take a deep breath, congratulate your team, and tomorrow be prepared to work hard to keep it great. If your intranet is not as effective as it could be, use the tools and resources in this book to figure out why it's stuck and how you can make it great – for your organization and your employees.

Tools

intranetsunstuck.com

TABLE OF CONTENTS

- Quiz
- 10 Reasons

STRATEGY

- Strategy Development Guide
- Standards and Guidelines
- Integration Guidelines

USERS

- User Interface Guide
- Employee Questionnaire

TECHNOLOGY

- IT Requirements Checklist

CONTENT

- Typical Intranet Content Categories
- Content Strategy Discussion Guide
- Content Consolidation Roadmap

RESOURCES

- Job Descriptions

COMMUNICATIONS

- Communication Plan

MEASUREMENT

- Annual Intranet Assessment Framework

ABOUT THE AUTHORS

Tracy Beverly

Tracy has 20 years' experience working with clients to develop and implement best-in-class intranets in support of business productivity and successful user experience. Eminently practical and detail-oriented, she focuses on content organization and quality, corporate information and communications, information architecture, regional/international/divisional management and governance, and real-world usability testing.

Tracy is a certified project manager with extensive international experience, sometimes working with 100+ countries on a single project. She has supported projects through implementation of new designs, new technologies, content management system migrations, and offshore development.

Early in her career she was Global Director of PricewaterhouseCoopers' KnowledgeCurve intranet, named by CIO to their Top Intranets list three years in a row. She has consulted to the URS Corporation's intranet since its inception in 2001 and continuing through three subsequent versions, the last of which was named to the Nielsen Best Intranet 2010 list.

Susan O'Neill

Susan O'Neill is a retired principal of PricewaterhouseCoopers (PwC), one of the world's largest professional services firms, and has more than twenty years of experience in leading and executing intranet and Internet strategies on a global level. Her experience as the leader of PwC's global web strategy included migrating more than 130 territory sites to a new UI and content strategy as well as technology platform. In addition, she drove the creation of the firm's global intranet, used by PwC employees in more than 100 territories.

At PwC, Susan successfully led multidisciplinary global teams with resources from various departments including Brand, Marketing, Knowledge Management, and IT.

Susan has worked with senior executives around the globe to develop and successfully execute business strategies dependent on effective integration of web technologies.

Edward Walter

Ed comes from a design background and has led teams in solving interface, usability and navigation problems inherent in the online space. He has worked with PricewaterhouseCoopers (originally Coopers & Lybrand) and Watson Wyatt Worldwide, ASME (American Society of Mechanical Engineers), Aetna Inc., Pfizer, Ernst & Young, Schlumberger, URS, Tyco and Lockheed Martin on collaboration tools, employee benefits programs, health portals, financial reporting platforms and other intranet-related projects.

Ed's work has been published widely, and he has delivered talks to business groups and universities both domestically and internationally. He is a faculty member of Parsons The New School for Design.

ACKNOWLEDGEMENTS

Susan, Tracy and I would first like to thank our families for their support and allowing us the time to write and put this book together. Additionally, we three owe a debt of gratitude to the entire staff at Strategy Studio and to our editor. Especially the help and skill provided by Simon Lugassy, William Reid and Nam Jae Yoon, and our editor, Charlie Marshall. Your contributions have been invaluable to us. Thank you all.

Edward Walter

www.ingramcontent.com/pod-product-compliance
Lightning Source LLC
Chambersburg PA
CBHW041932220326
41598CB00055BA/27